ENTOURAGE

ENTOURAGE

A Tracing File and Color Sourcebook

4th Edition

Ernest Burden

McGraw-Hill
New York Chicago San Francisco
Lisbon London Madrid Mexico City
Milan New Delhi San Juan Seoul
Singapore Sydney Toronto

The McGraw-Hill Companies

Cataloging-in-Publication Data is on file with the Library of Congress.

    3 4 5 6 7 8 9 0   QPD/QPD   0 9 8 7 6 5

ISBN 0-07-140724-3

The sponsoring editor of this book was Cary Sullivan, the editing supervisor was Steven Melvin, and the production supervisor was Sherri Souffrance.

Printed and bound by Quebecor/Dubuque.

McGraw-Hill books are available at special quantity discounts to use as premiums and sales promotions, or for use in corporate training programs. For more information, please write to the Director of Special Sales, McGraw-Hill Professional's, Two Penn Plaza, New York, NY 10121-2298. Or contact your local bookstore.

This book was printed on recycled, acid-free paper containing a minimum of 50% recycled, de-inked fiber.

Acknowledgments

This book represents the efforts of many people on the production side, as well as those on the artistic side, mentioned in the credits for drawings.

A special thanks to my editor, Cary Sullivan, who suggested a new look for this edition, and to Scott Grillo, who encouraged the addition of color images for this edition. Tom Kowalczyk expertly handled the production of this edition, as he has done with all previous editions.

Thanks to Margaret Webster-Shapiro for her contribution to the production of a stunning cover, designed by Jeff McKay of 3r1 Group.

A very special thanks to my wife Joy, for her unending encouragement throughout; especially during the final production of this edition.

CONTENTS

Drawing Credits

This book represents a unique combination of artistic talent and photographic technique. I am grateful for the artistic contribution of my daughter Analisa, my son Ernest III, and my friend Brian Burr, whose work appeared in all previous editions of this book.

Analisa's drawings are found on pages 26, 27, and 31 - 34.
Ernest's drawings are found on pages 30, 35, 36, 77, 83, 85, 90, 97, and 99.
Brian Burr's drawings are found on pages 28, 29, 45 - 55, 64 – 67, 72, 75, 89, and Title pages 346 – 347.
The fireworks photos on page 376 are by Joy Arnold (Burden).

I am also grateful for the talented work of the late Robert McIlhargy and his wife Lori Brown, who supplied many splendid examples featuring the use of entourage in professional renderings. Thanks also to all the talented delineators whose rendering examples enhance this edition. They are:

J. Henderson Barr, Stanley Doctor, Robert and Anna Fisher, Richard Gardner, Gordon Grice, Andy Hickes, Ron Love, Mark DeNalovy Rozvadovski, and Walter Thomason.

The illustration of the atrium on the cover is by Ernest burden III, done for Robert A. M. Stern, architects, New York.

Most architecture schools offer a disproportionate number of courses on the basics of design and drafting, and not enough emphasis on the presentation of those designs. Hence, when students become licensed professionals, they find that they must rely on others to assist them in this vital area. Most professional delineators begin their training in architecture, and later specialize in presentation drawing. Only a handful of people have studied architectural illustration at college level, in preparation for a career in perspective drawing. Most have acquired the skill for drawing along the way in their training or job experience.

An artist's sketch of a scene or a building is a personal interpretation, and the skill in perceiving the object and the technique of drawing it is the only criterion for its success. This is not so with an architectural illustration. Producing a perspective view is a technical matter; either it's right, or it's wrong. The building or interior must be accurately depicted from one particular vantage point in space.

Perspective layouts can be sketched without the use of instruments, but they serve only as an approximation, mainly for viewpoint selection. True perspectives are mechanically plotted using the principles of projection developed during the Renaissance.

Perspective layouts can also be produced by photographing models, or "stage-set props," to allow a more accurate representation from an infinite number of vantage points. Once a model of the project is built in the computer, it can also display and plot an infinite number of perspective vantage points and a range of views, including some that are not possible to obtain using the camera. However, the end product of all these different approaches must be the same; that is, to produce a realistic representation of how the project will appear when it is completed.

Material in this book was derived from thousands of photographs taken from countless sources worldwide. They were selected for their strict appropriateness to professional architectural and interior illustration. In addition, photographs were collected from publications, advertisements, and catalogs, and traced into line drawings.

Drawings were made from these sources eliminating all but the most necessary details. In some cases, backgrounds behind the images were masked out, leaving just the figure. However, don't let the accuracy of this material inhibit you. The drawings can be traced over directly, or interpreted in your own drawing style and technique, using any medium you desire.

Most people can accomplish a good layout by using one of the methods described earlier. However, not everyone has the ability to draw the entourage in the proper size and proportion without some reference material for guidance. Therefore, this book offers decades of experience in the collection and use of entourage images, based on the author's own working files, and those of other professional delineators.

The format of this book is like that of a portfolio, wherein the front and back of each page exists separately from the rest of the book. The pages can be removed from the book along the perforations, and filed according to your individual needs. Once removed, the pages are designed with an inner margin to accommodate a three-hole punch, allowing for storage in a binder for easy access.

The true measure of effectiveness of any drawing file is fast retrieval. With a poor system, you can spend many hours searching for the right figure, tree, or vehicle. In this book, the different types and species of entourage are conveniently categorized. They are further subdivided within each category according to size or type of activity.

All the drawings are reproduced for tracing directly into your drawing. They are shown in the most commonly used sizes and scales. However, you can easily enlarge or reduce any of the illustrations on a photocopier in small increments for specific use. If you prefer to leave the book intact, you can photocopy the desired pages. If you photocopy them onto acetate sheets, you can use them either as left-reading or right-reading images. Some copiers can automatically produce such a "mirror image."

The illustrations can be scanned into a computer, and then manipulated in a variety of ways, depending on the software program used. They can be put onto their own separate "layer," so that they do not affect the rest of the drawing, and then they can be combined in the final printout.

You can build your own file of images in your computer for ease of use. The techniques available today within numerous software programs for altering graphics and illustrations will add variety to this material. This will contribute to the enhancement of your drawings and give your work a professional quality.

INTRODUCTION

There are many different sources from which to derive designs for use in your drawings as the elements of entourage. They range from the ready-made to the customized versions that you produce yourself. The sources include published print material as well as many software templates and CD images. They all have very specific advantages and disadvantages, not only in their makeup, but in their use and appropriateness to your drawing. The serious user will search among all the available sources, since there is something to gain from each one. It is the task of the perspective artist to select the proper element for the drawing.

The most accessible source is from periodicals that fill the stores each month. The articles and advertisements are almost always illustrated with photographs of people and vehicles in a variety of unusual situations and viewpoints. They may include exotic locations and camera angles impossible to achieve by yourself. The cost to get these unusual images is relatively low. However, you may have to search through many pages before finding any to use. You should cut them out even if you don't have an immediate use for them, and create a file for each situation. This is the beginning of a "clip-art" file, which is the backbone of every commercial artist's resources.

The next most obvious source is printed catalogs, which are specifically designed to feature the item in a controlled way. There are fashion and retail sales catalogs for clothes, manufacturers' catalogs for new vehicles, and furniture manufacturers' catalogs for furnishings. They are all excellent sources for specific images.

You will find a wide range of styles and the latest fashions, with ready-to-use poses if you select them carefully. You have to remember that they are set up to feature the clothes, and such things as dramatic lighting or unusual camera angles may render them inappropriate for your use. In any case, they are excellent material for reference, even if they cannot be traced exactly to fit your prescribed angle of perspective.

Another source for images is the daily or weekly newspaper, which contains many advertisements for fashions and vehicles. These images are printed using line illustrations or other graphic conversions rather than photographs. As such, the images are lower in quality than magazine or catalog images, and more difficult to store in a file, due to their impermanent nature.

The most accurate and appropriate images will probably be the ones that you create yourself. You choose your own location, your own subject, and your own timing. You choose your own perspective angles when photographing vehicles, and your own species when photographing trees.

The disadvantage to doing it yourself is the difficulty in getting the unusual viewpoints, especially aerial views. The other difficulty is separating your subject from the background. In many catalogs, backgrounds and viewpoints are selected so as not to be a distraction. Airbrushing or masking removes any of the remaining distracting elements.

For the commercial artist there are many publications called "pose files," featuring figures in a variety of unusual situations. Some of these contain the same situation depicted in a series of rotated views and adjusted camera angles. Most often these are outside the situations needed for an architectural scene, where standard street, or eye-level viewpoints are the most desirable. Many figures in these series are posed in the nude as well.

New and affordable hardware has spawned a variety of software programs that allow images to be stored and combined electronically. Many programs are offered with clip-art "add-ons." The most recent format for these images is the CD, in which thousands of color images can be stored until you decide to use them. You import only the images you want while preserving valuable storage space.

The color images require a very large database and internal memory to use, and require a lot of time to plot out or to render into your drawing. These are two-dimensional images that are supported mainly in TIFF files, and used in various software programs. Others are in much smaller JPEG files, which are more than adequate for rendering use.

For three-dimensional work, such as solid modeling or computer animation "walk-throughs," there are templates or three-dimensional "blocks" for figures, vehicles, and landscape designs. These are fully scalable and can be rotated in any direction to fit the exact prescribed perspective angle of your drawing. These blocks are loaded from CDs and require a large database to accept and use these files. These images are composed of three-dimensional vertices, and as such can be rendered, or "texture-mapped" with a variety of materials and colors, all of which are available in the same software programs.

Once you have selected any of the images from the sources mentioned, you have to decide how to get them into a usable form for your drawings. There are several techniques to use, depending on your desired end result and the need for accuracy in your drawing.

The most common usage is to trace the image directly, using an ink pen on acetate for maximum clarity. If the image is drawn on a clear acetate sheet, it can easily be turned over for a reverse-reading image. Matte acetate can also be used, as well as heavyweight tracing paper. The advantage to this method of tracing is that the image will be drawn in your own hand and will match the style of the rest of the drawing. Another advantage is that you need only trace those items that you want, omitting distracting backgrounds or unnecessary details within the figure itself.

A more exact replica of the image can be obtained by using a photocopy machine to produce a graphic interpretation of the image. This is accomplished with a feature now built into many digitizing copiers that allows you to produce an automatically traced "outline" of the image. Many computer software programs have a similar outline or "auto-trace" feature, which finds the edges of shapes and traces a line around them. The procedure to accomplish this is similar when using a photocopier or the computer.

First, you have to convert the photograph into a high-contrast or gray-scale image. Then the trace feature will precisely outline all the black areas. If you do not convert it first, the outline feature will not know which tones to trace, and the resulting image will be very erratic. There are more options in the computer for converting the image into one that is easier for the outline feature to recognize, such as the controls for the gray-scale and contrast.

Many of these techniques can be accomplished with a digitizing photocopy machine quite easily and inexpensively. Many of the outline images shown in this book were produced by the simple photocopy method described. The result is an image that looks like it was drawn by hand, yet retains all the accuracy of the original photograph. This technique works particularly well for the rendition of trees, plants, and other foliage.

PART 1
■ Layouts

The overlay sketch is useful in helping to establish just the right balance of activity, and to focus the attention toward the center of interest, by placing large foreground figures looking into the drawing from either side. The intended use of the space will help to determine the gender mix of figures, the dress, and many other details. Each of the figures should be dressed appropriately for the intended function and season of the year. The proper use of these entourage images will enhance the overall success of the drawing in every way.

The human figure has been used throughout the history of artistic representation as a device for creating a sense of activity, and establishing scale within a scene. The first stage in the rendition of these figures usually consists of a loosely scribbled sketch, defining the location and mass of the figure. This allows flexibility in the early stages of a layout. Later they can be replaced with more developed figures, which can be drawn on an overlay of tracing paper or acetate.

Placing this arrangement of figures under a tracing paper original allows you to draw them directly into the drawing. However, if you are working on an opaque board, you will have to first transfer the figures to the board. This is done by placing a carbon sheet behind the figures and tracing over them, then finishing them in the final medium.

On interior scenes, the scale of the figures is extremely important. An overlay sketch is a useful tool to study how to indicate the right amount of activity within the room. The intended function of the room will determine the proper mix of standing, seated, or walking figures. The use of large-scale figures in the foreground help give depth to the interior space. Each figure should be dressed in a style and fashion that is appropriate to the use of the room, whether it is intended for business, casual or commercial activities.

It is the elements of entourage that give special meaning and presence to a rendering of a space, particularly if it involves any specific activities. These elements include special dress or accessories, graphics and signage, furniture, fixtures, and all types of exterior environmental elements.

For exterior scenes, you may need to depict a certain climate or activity, such as a beach resort or a winter scene. Here the appropriate demeanor, activity and dress of the figures will enhance the drawing to a great degree. Buildings or interior spaces are not meant to exist in a vacuum, devoid of life and activity. By indicating the vitality of the space with the proper selection of the elements of entourage, the drawing will become alive, and hence more successful.

PART 2
■ Figures

Part 2 FIGURES

In an architectural rendering we must be just as concerned with the accurate representation of the human figure as any other artistic form of communication, such as commercial illustration. Figures bring life and a sense of scale to any drawing. Scale is one of the more important aspects in relating the building to its environment, and the elements of entourage help to establish the building within its context. The easiest way to get these elements is to photograph them in a natural environment, preferably within the context of the actual project site.

Photographing people is a relatively easy matter, and any hand-held camera will suffice. It's best to use a high-speed film, with a rating of 400 ASA. The subject is generally walking, and you will want to stop any action with a fast shutter speed, while maintaining a depth of field to keep the subject in focus.

Photographing people in public spaces is preferable to photographing them on a sidewalk, where a strong directional element is present. The open area of a park or plaza will give you more room and opportunity for getting a wider variety of poses. In one afternoon you could get enough material for many months of rendering use. The easiest method is to use a "point- and-shoot" camera, since it will automatically advance the film. This allows you to concentrate on the movement of the figures, as you do not have to look away from the viewfinder. The camera should also have a zoom feature so that you can frame the figure to fill the viewfinder. This allows you to control the framing of distant figures. It is much easier to deal with a large figure than a small one, especially when converting or scanning the photograph into a drawing, as there will be more detail on the image.

Keep in mind that people photograph heavier than they really are, and that clothes add bulk to the figure. Pictures taken on a bright sunny day will have much higher contrast, and details in the shadowed areas may become obscured. Therefore, overcast days are best for getting the maximum amount of detail.

Using photography as the basis for the image of the figure has many merits. If you do not like the pose, you can alter it to suit your needs. You can add or subtract details or textures, you can even change the figures to be taller or shorter in most imaging software programs, and on some digital photocopying machines. Even the most commonplace photocopy machine has a zoom function that can enlarge and reduce the image, which changes the scale of the figure. Even if you alter the figure, you will still have an accurate photographic base.

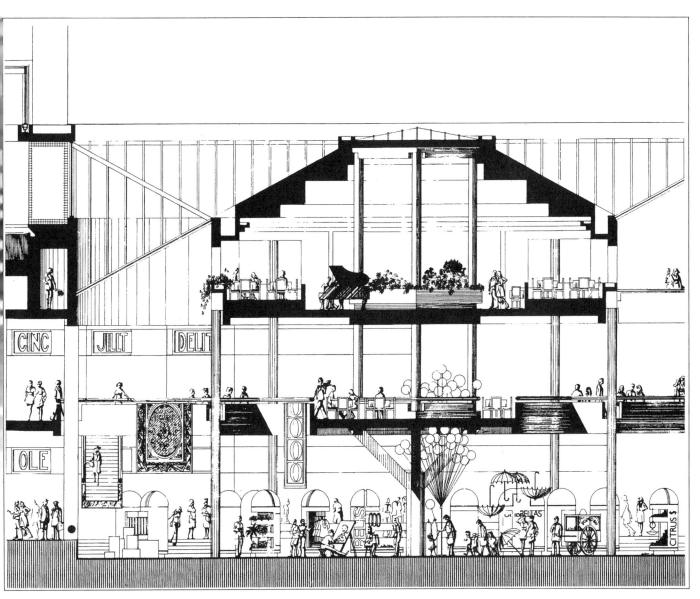

■ People exist in all shapes and sizes but average measurements have been developed which allow us to design useful tools and buildings for human activities. These standards are extremely important to the industrial designer, the interior designer, and the architect. They all need measurable references as to how the designs will be inhabited by the end user. The same is true of an architectural or interior design drawing. It must be drawn to a conventional scale, and a way to indicate that is to add human figures at the same scale as the drawing.

FIGURES: Female - 1/2" Scale

FIGURES: Female - 3/8" Scale

FIGURES: Couples - 1/4" Scale **39**

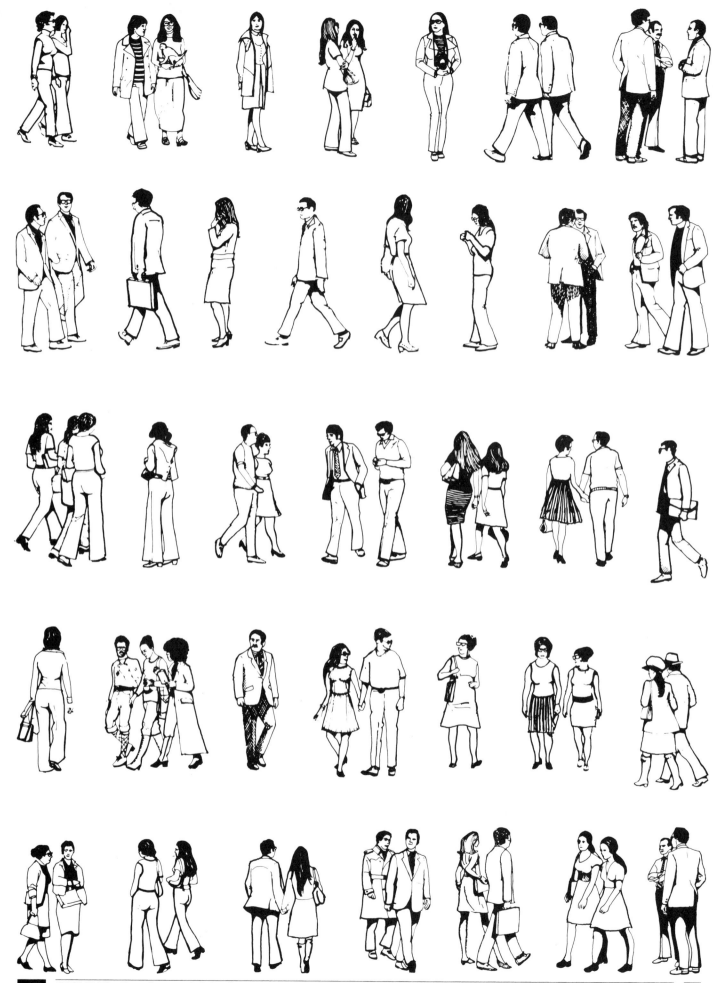

Once we leave orthographic floor plans, elevations, and sections, we enter the three-dimensional representation of physical space on a two-dimensional surface. We need objects in the space to help create the sense of depth and perspective, and the use of human figures is an excellent device for illustrating depth. By varying the size of these figures, we can create the illusion of distance and perspective diminution. At the same time, the tonal rendition of the figures helps create movement, and adds a sense of depth and reality to the drawing.

FIGURES: Male / Large

Our drawings would be pretty dull and lifeless if we only showed a solitary figure within a space. Groups of figures and families will add a more realistic atmosphere, provided that it is appropriate to the function of the space. The use of children within these groups, or by themselves, requires additional study to be accurate, and appropriate to the activity. Children are not just small versions of adults. They have their own characteristics, such as a larger head in relation to the body, and different proportions among other body parts.

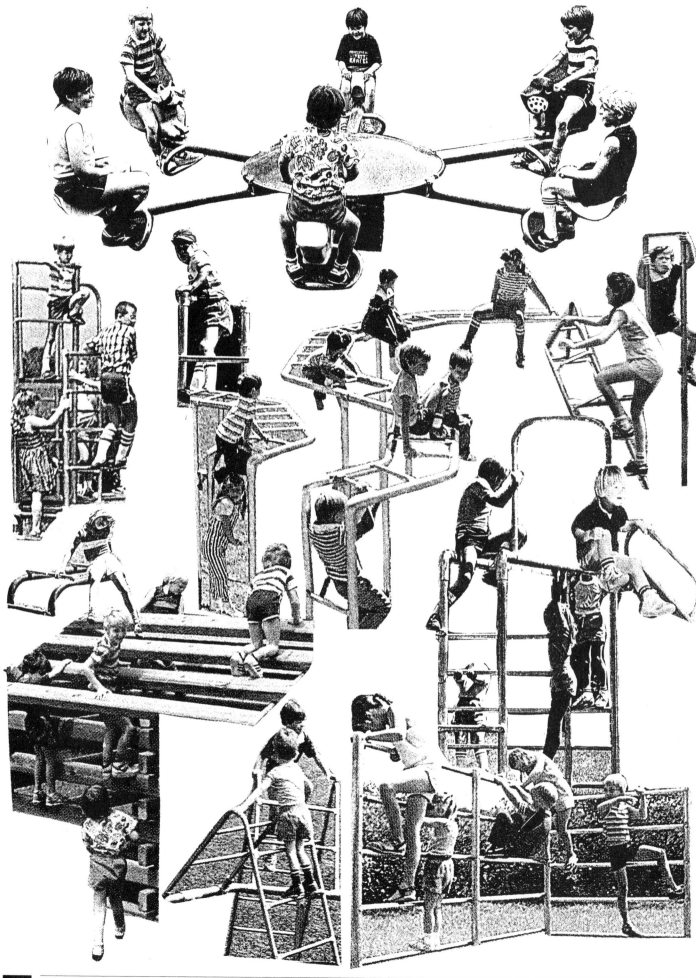

FIGURES: Children / Playground

There are many projects that have very specific functional uses, such as airports, hospitals, shopping center malls, and other hospitality functions. Certainly there will be architectural features that describe these functions, but they can be greatly enhanced in the presentation stage. By carefully selecting these special figures you can illustrate the functional use of the space very easily. Every item in the drawing will then relate to the theme, and the addition of graphics, signage, and appropriate fixtures will add to this specially created ambience.

FIGURES: Native Dress

■ Seated figures are often difficult to draw without reference material, as the figure is usually bent over or partially concealed. Place all the standing figures at eye level and the seated ones proportionately lower, unless the eye level is at the seated level. Seated figures used on the edge of a drawing will frame it nicely, but should be placed so that they are looking back into the drawing. Since the viewer will look in the same direction that the figure is looking, you can use them as a main element in composing the drawing.

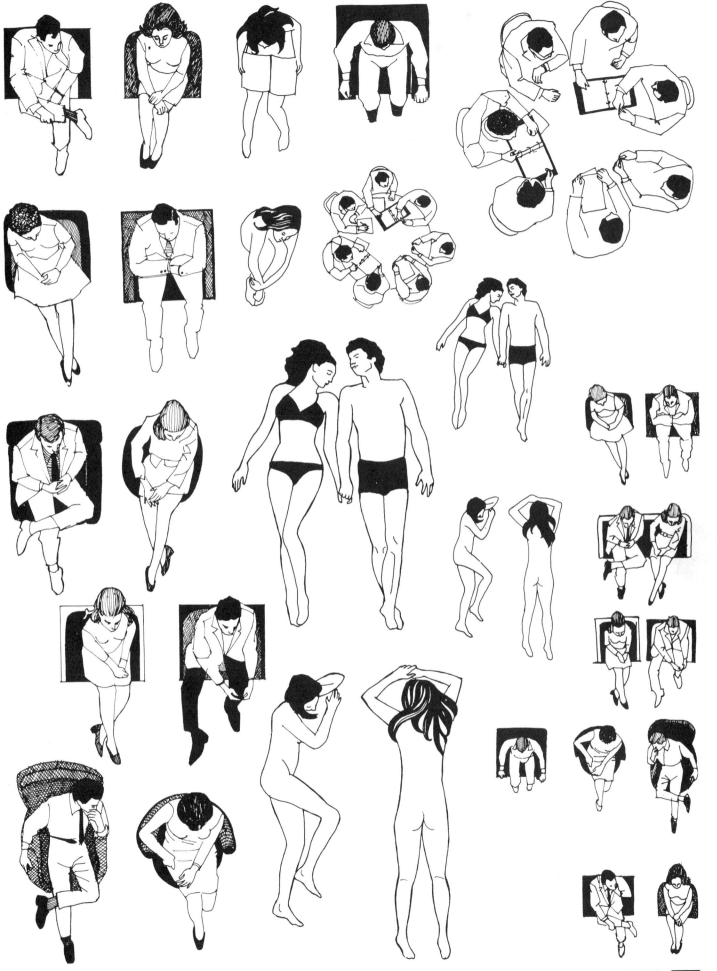

■ Many residential projects feature some ancillary recreational functions, which are highlighted in sales brochures and other promotional documents. Some projects are directly related to sports activities by their function; like summer and winter resorts, and certain retail stores. Figures used for these facilities should highlight the movement and activity associated with the active sports; running, riding, cycling, skating, and playing tennis and golf. The proper use of figures that depict those activities enhances the drawing, and gives it spontaneity.

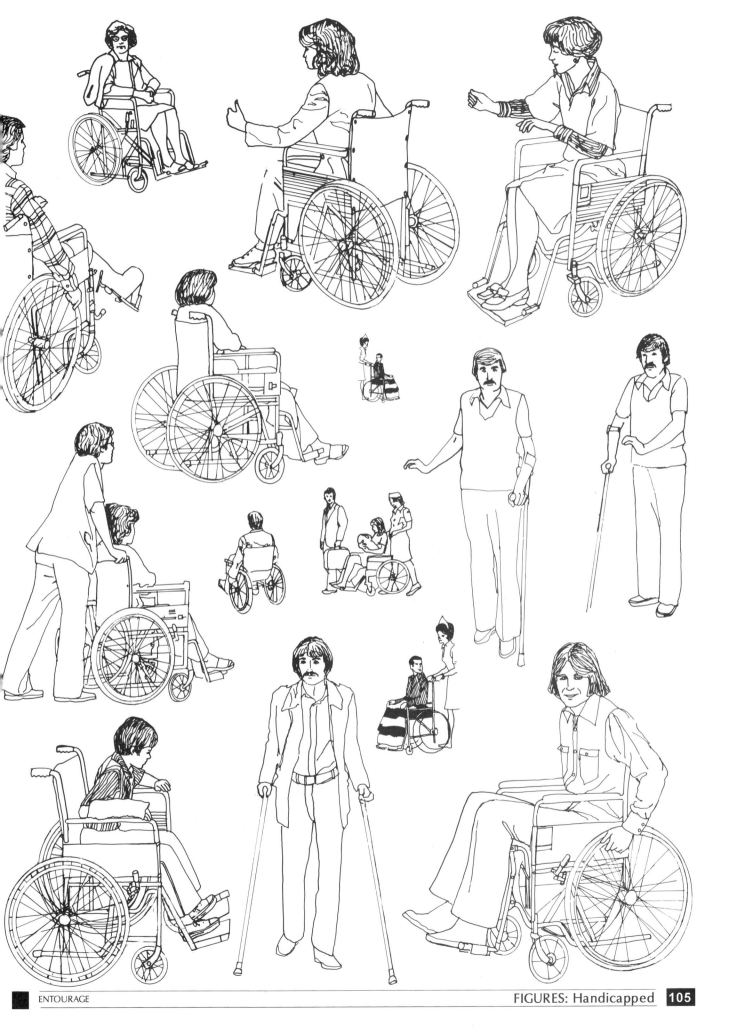

■ Since photography is the basis of all the figures in this book, many can be used in this original form. Therefore, the figures are not retouched. Only the distracting backgrounds have been eliminated. Certain photos were digitized, outlined, and reproduced for two purposes. The first is to use them directly in your drawings by cutting and pasting, or by scanning into your computer right out of the book. The second is to provide a resource for you to trace in your own hand, and to render in your own technique, using your own preferred medium.

The term "photo-drawing" is used to describe any process where photography and drawing are combined in the same document. This technique can produce a very realistic representation combined with an artistic one. A photograph of the scene, taken from the desired vantage point, is the basis for the drawing. Certain parts of the original photograph may be incorporated directly into the drawing, and other parts may be added as needed.

While at the scene, take lots of extra photographs of people or additional objects. When these are inserted into the drawing, they will all have the same lighting conditions. These figures can then be cut out of the photograph and the edges blackened with a felt-tip pen to hide the white cut edges. These figures or objects are then simply pasted onto the original photograph, as in a photo-montage. This entire paste-up can then be re-photographed for a smooth copy.

The drawing of the new project may be done in any medium. If it is done directly on the photograph, any opaque medium, such as tempera can be used. If done on a different surface, any medium can be used, and the image can be cut out and pasted onto the photograph. The final paste-up can be retouched and then re-photographed for the finished product. The identical technique can work for either black and white or color images. The end result is one of accuracy and realism, combined with an artistic touch.

The decision to do a site coordinated photodrawing in this instance, came from a need to show an existing, recognizable bas-relief sculpture on an adjacent building. Several photos were taken during class hours, but the payoff came when students came out to change classes.

When the photos were developed it was clear that the best representation of the project would be to render the building into the photograph, rather than paste pictures of the students into the rendering. This would provide the maximum sense of realism, and would show the sculpture to the best advantage.

The building was drawn separately and reduced to the proper size, and cut out and pasted into the photograph. Then additional photographs of individual students were strategically placed into the photograph over the rendered builkding to provide additional depth and realism.

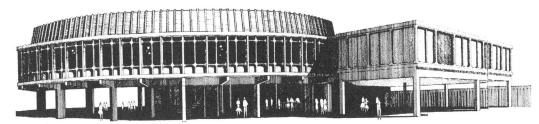

The images printed in this book are all reproduced with the highest quality, color balance, and resolution. This allows them to be scanned by the user, and re-positioned within a plan, elevation, sketch, or finished rendering. The process is much easier than scanning your own images, in that the tedious work of masking the image from its background is already done for you in most cases. This is particularly useful for the images of trees and plants, where masking of individual leaves is very time consuming.

When scanning the images directly from the book, choose either a bitmap file for the black and white images, or full color for the color images. Select a size approximately equal to the size of the final image in the finished drawing. This will keep the file size down to a minimum. Select a resolution that will be compatible with the rest of the drawing. Use 1200–2400 dpi for high-resolution enlargements or printing. A lower resolution of 100–300 dpi will be suitable for most rendering work.

Once the scanned image is imported into Photoshop, or any other software program, you should examine the following items under the "Image" menu. First, check the "Adjust" functions; i.e., color balance, brightness / contrast, and hue / saturation, to make sure it fits with the tone and values of the rest of your drawing.

Next, under the same "Image" menu, check the "Size" function, which lets you control the dimensions and the resolution. Finally, under the "Filter" menu, you will be able to alter the image with certain artistic effects, such as "Pencil" and "Watercolor." You will also be able to soften or enhance the image with the "Blur," or "Sharpen" function.

Under the same filter menu, you will find the "Stylize" function, which leads you to the "Trace contour" function mentioned

earlier. There are many other special effects available under this menu, but some are outside the normal requirements for rendering use.

Once you have made all of the adjustments to the image that are desired, you have to create a transparent background for all of the areas outside of your image. Copying the image directly will include an accompanying rectangle around the image. A "clipping path" lets you isolate the image and make everything outside of it transparent when you place it in another application.

First, create a "clipping path" around the image from the "Paths palette" menu, then copy the selected image. There are two ways to accomplish this. The "Save" command saves the image in its current state as a Photoshop file format. The "Save As" command lets you save an alternate version with a different name. When scanning images that have white or light colors at the edge of the image, the clipping path may follow the denser part of the image, and the white area may also become transparent.

To modify the shape of a clipping path, you must first select the path name in the "Paths" palette to display the path. The path is displayed as a series of anchor points connected by a series of straight lines.

You can access this path and move the anchor points through the "Direct – Selection" function. "Direction" points appear as filled circles, "Selected" anchor points as filled squares, and "Unselected" anchor points as hollow squares. You can move these points by positioning the arrow pointer over an anchor point and pressing "Ctrl" (Windows) or "Command" (Mac OS). Sub-paths are selected by pressing "Alt/Option-clicking," and second sub-paths selected by holding down "Shift" and "Alt/Option-clicking." However, it will rarely be necessary to do these maneuvers.

A photo-entourage file is useful for other purposes than the application of a photo-drawing. By using a software paint program in the computer, you can alter the final technique of the rendering. First, the photos are scanned in at a moderately low-end resolution suitable for graphic images (100 - 300 dpi), rather than the high-end resolutions required for photo-realistic rendering (600 - 1200 dpi). This low-resolution image takes up far less disk space, and the images are going to be altered later anyway.

The next step is to turn the images into a graphic form. To do this you have to reduce the images either to a gray scale or line art illustration. Then you can produce a traced outline of the figure very easily. If the image is changed into a reversed image you can see the areas that have to be retouched before turning it into the positive trace outline shown here.

Other things can be done with any imported color image. You can apply any of the special effects in the software program you're using to create a pastel, conte crayon, or watercolor technique (as in the sample here). Using these new techniques will add a very professional appearance to your drawing.

The drawings on the following page were done totally inside the computer. The figures were scanned and put on a separate layer from the background drawing. This way they can be moved around easily without disturbing the drawing underneath.

The quality that can be achieved by this two-dimensional method of computer rendering is very impressive. It can exhibit the realism of most complex three-dimensional rendering techniques with only a fraction of the time and money invested in the drawing.

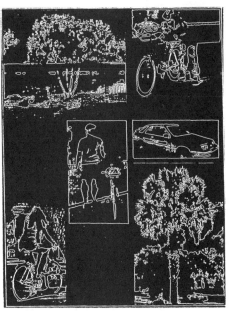

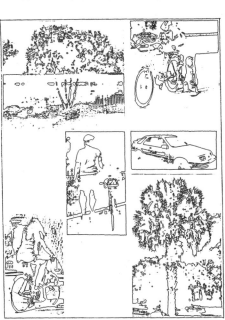

ANDY HICKES
NYC

FIGURES: Photos / Couples

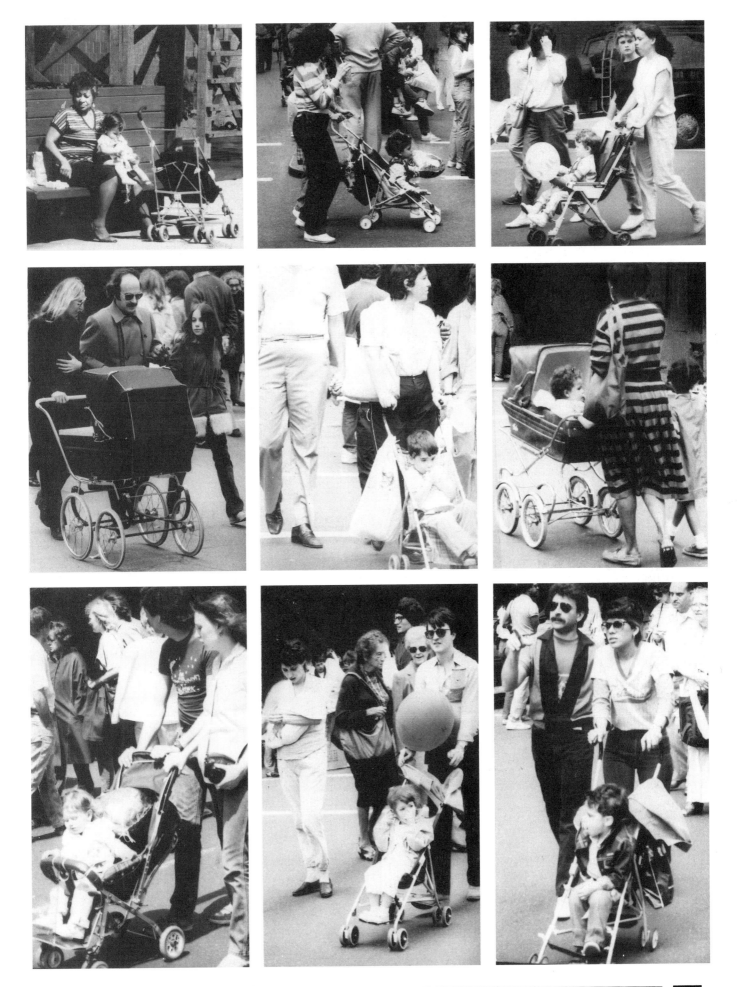

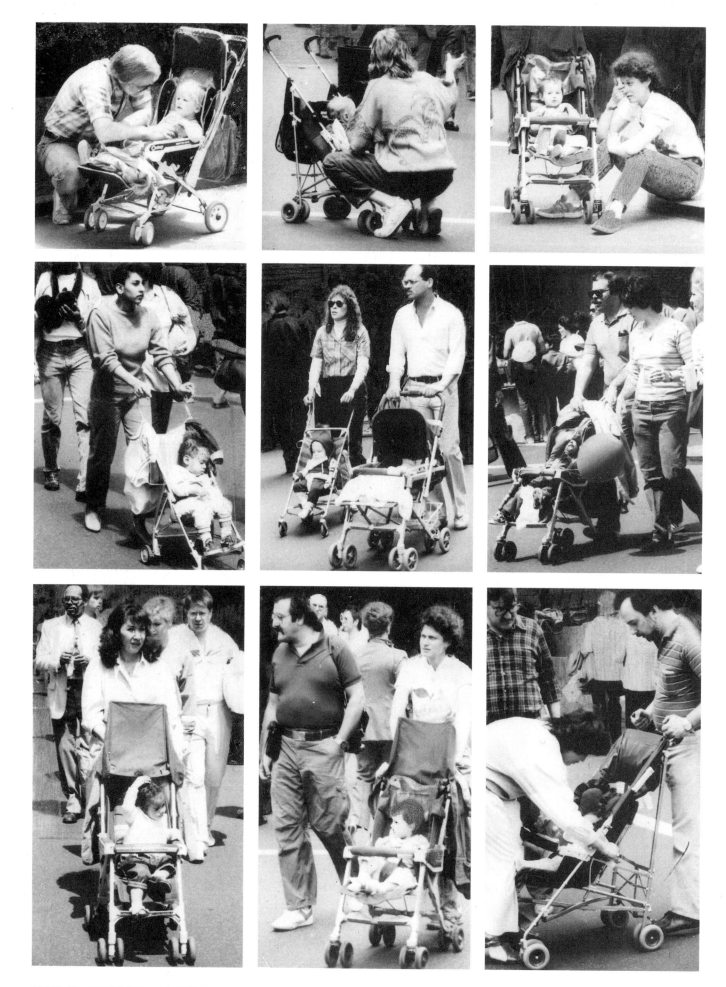

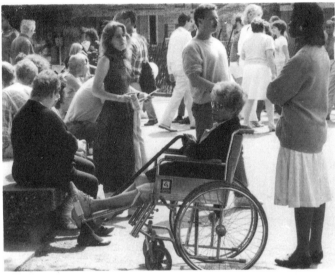

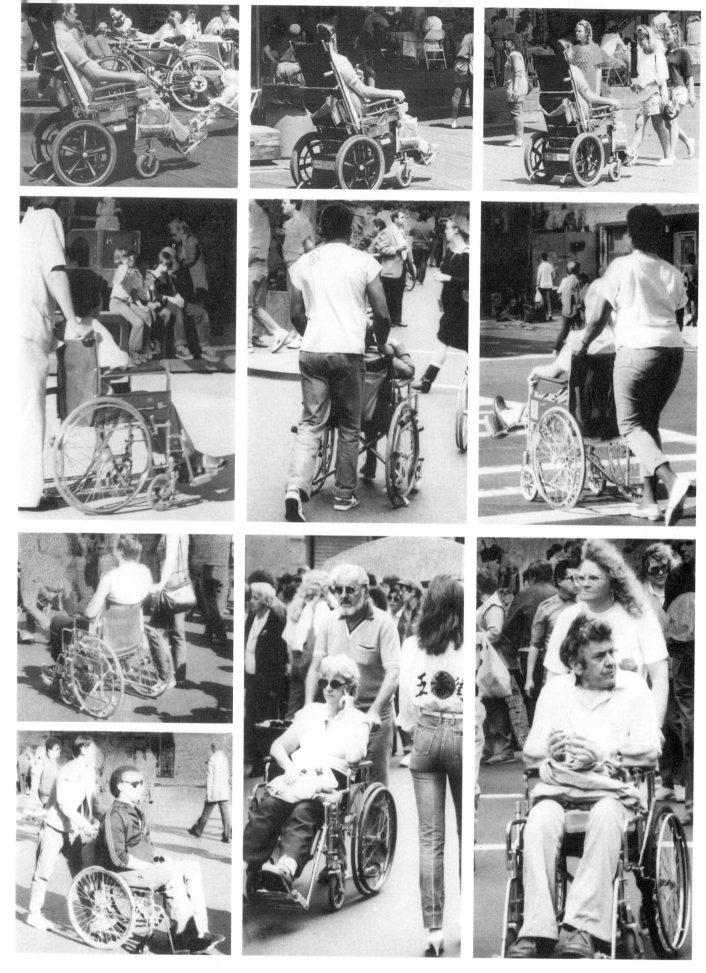

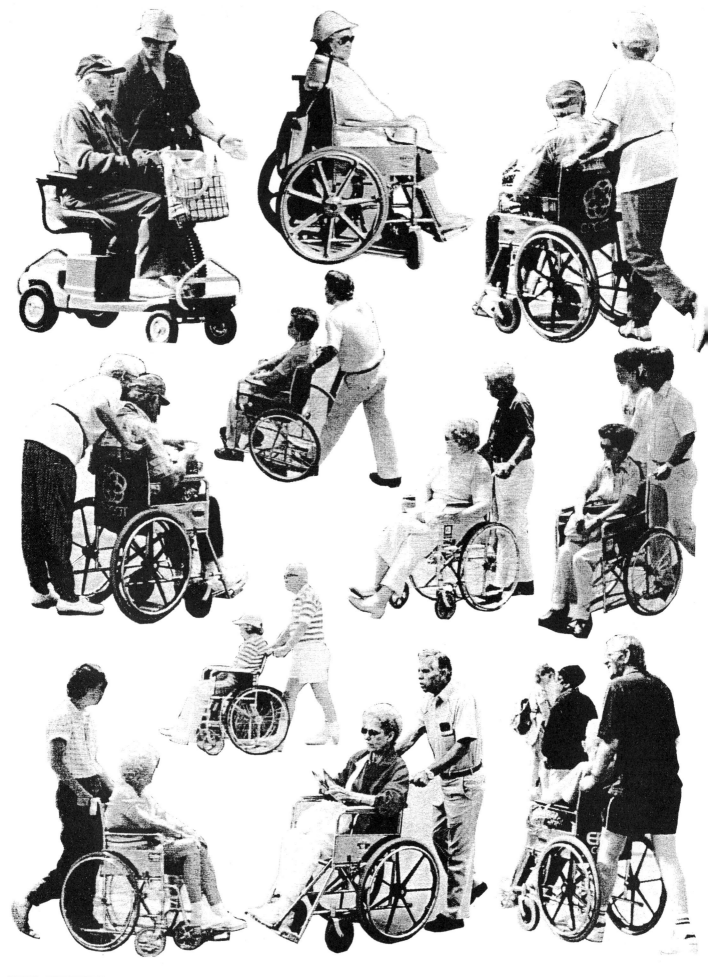

FIGURES: Photographs / Seated

FIGURES: Photos / Seated **157**

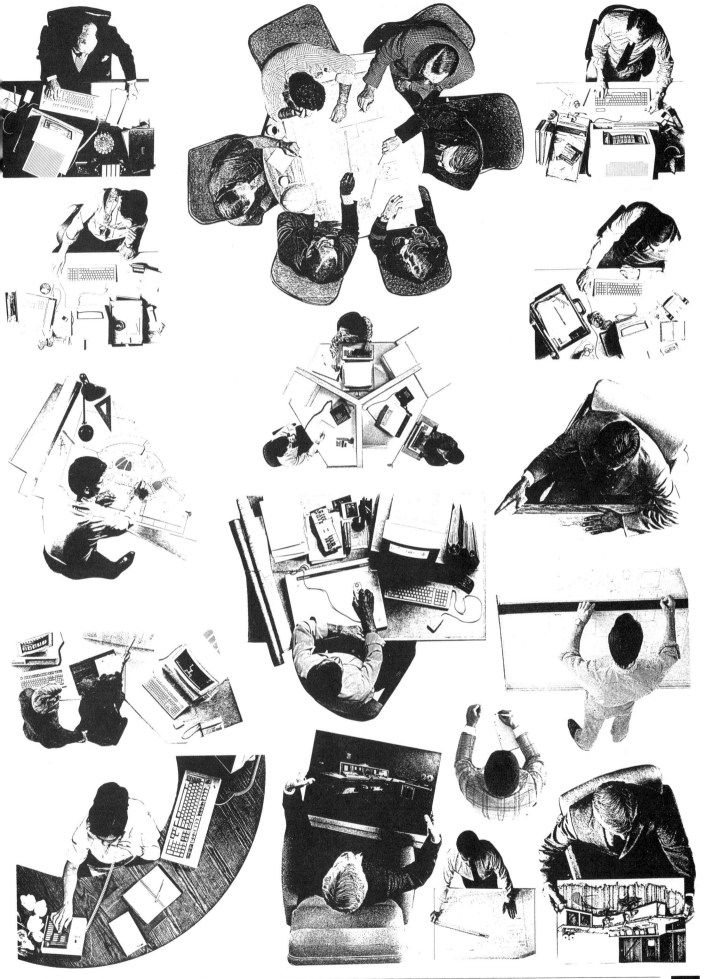

FIGURES: Couples / Casual **177**

FIGURES: Couples / Dressy **179**

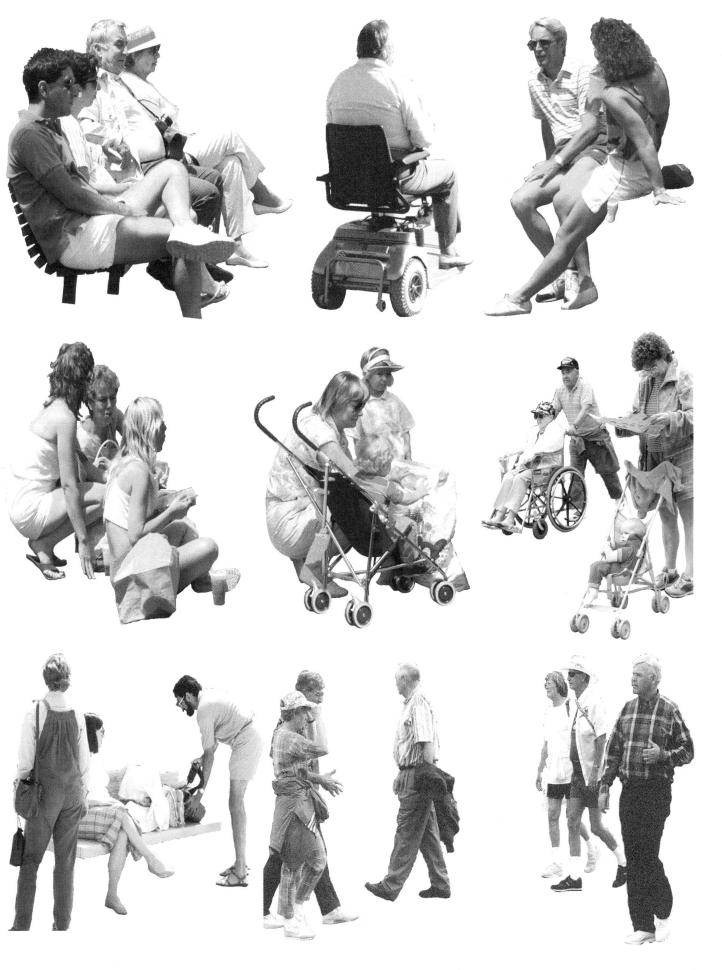

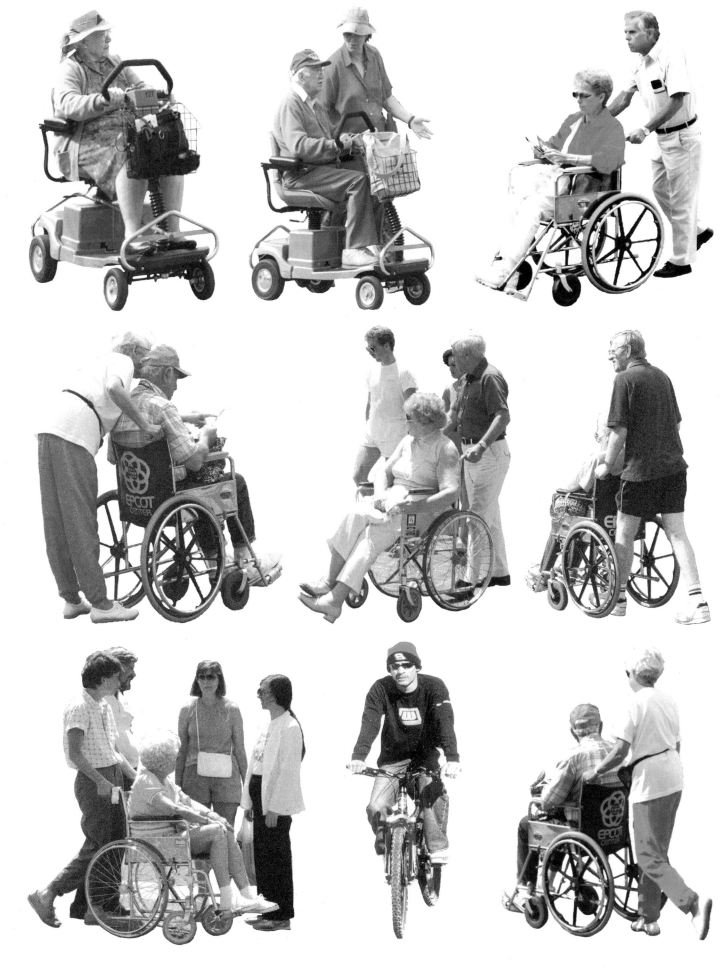

PART 3
■ Flora

© SLUTSKY & ASSOC. '88

A common element on a site plan is an overhead designation of a tree or group of trees. While the simplified form of a tree in plan view is an irregular outline approximating a circle, there are many variations on this pattern. Getting an overhead view of a tree is not an easy matter when out in the open, but there are many ways to see trees from above if you inside an atrium, which are commonplace today.

There are several other methods to study the shape of trees in plan view. One such method is to observe the shape of the shadow cast by a tree. At certain times of the day this would resemble its projected shape in plan. Another method is to photograph a portion of a tree that projects overhead, by pointing the camera straight up the tree. Use a wide-angle lens to get the most image from this close distance. Take a series of three or four pictures rotating around the trunk of the tree and later paste all the prints together using the trunk at the center.

On taller trees, such as palms, you can get the entire branch structure within one picture. Using the outline and scale of the branches or fronds, you can come up with an approximation of what the tree looks like from above. Although this does not provide you with the same full shape as a view from above, it gives you the proper scale and pattern of the branches to work from.

One of the most commonly used items in a site plan of a building, or a floor plan of a residential development, is a representation in plan view of trees, shrubs, and plants. They have usually been represented as an irregular circle with a dot in the center, or as more complex designs showing the branches and leaves. There is no standard symbol that fits all trees, therefore photographs will provide you with the correct size and shape. Then it is up to each individual artist to develop his or her own style and technique in depicting them.

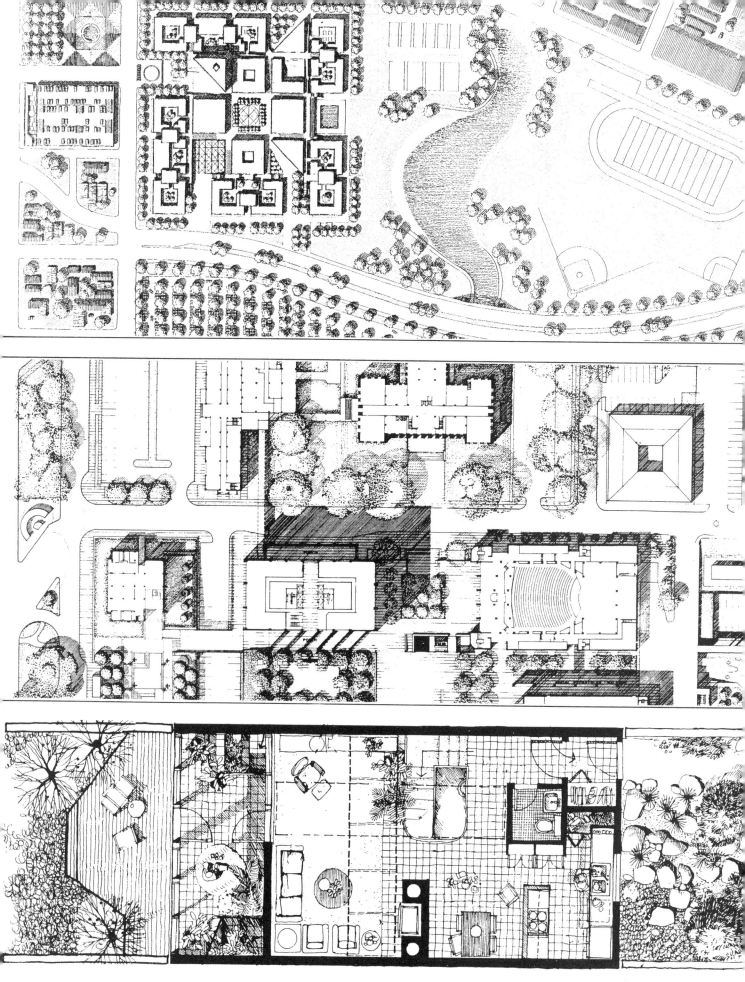

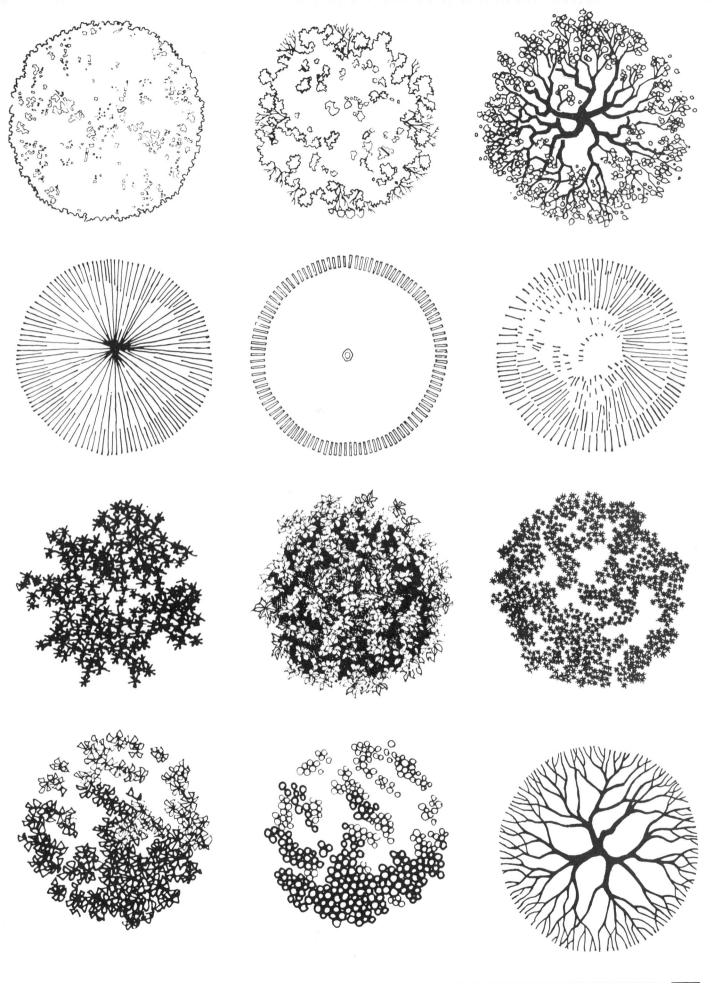

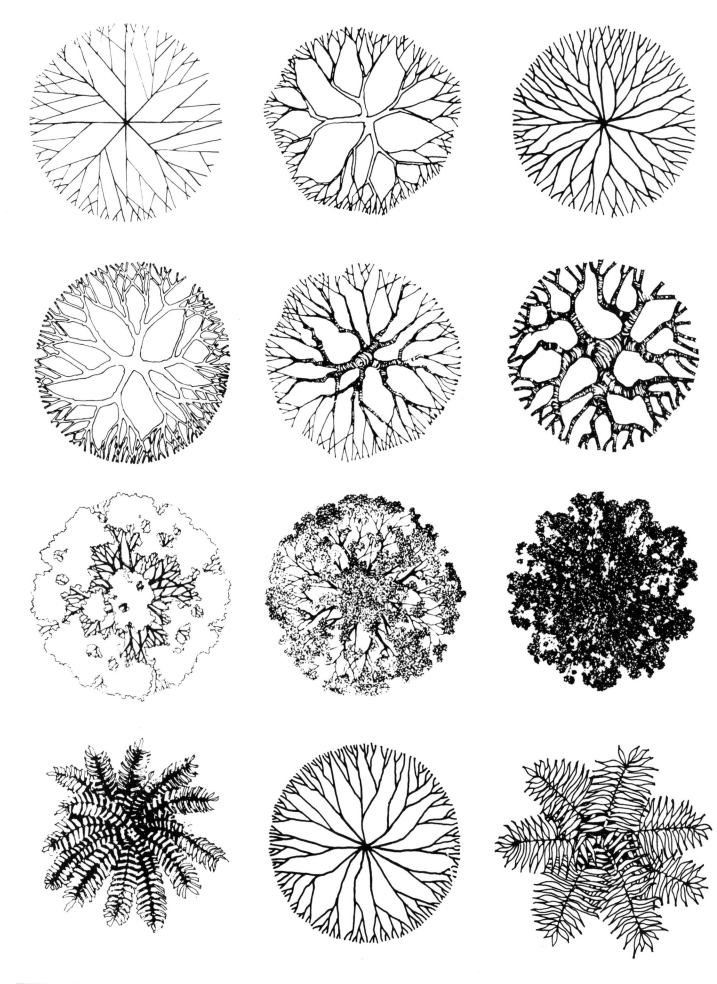

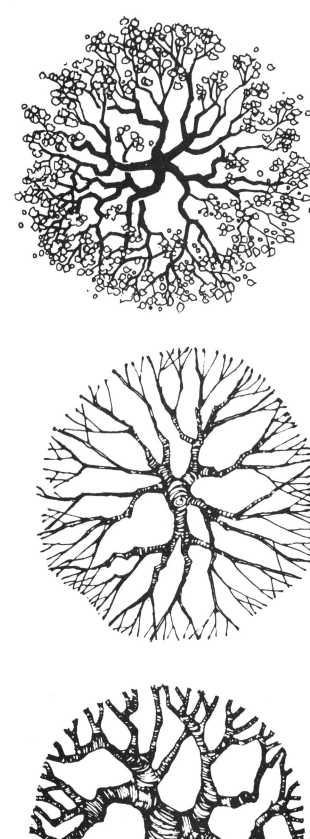
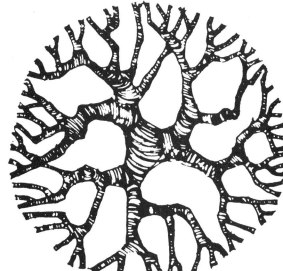

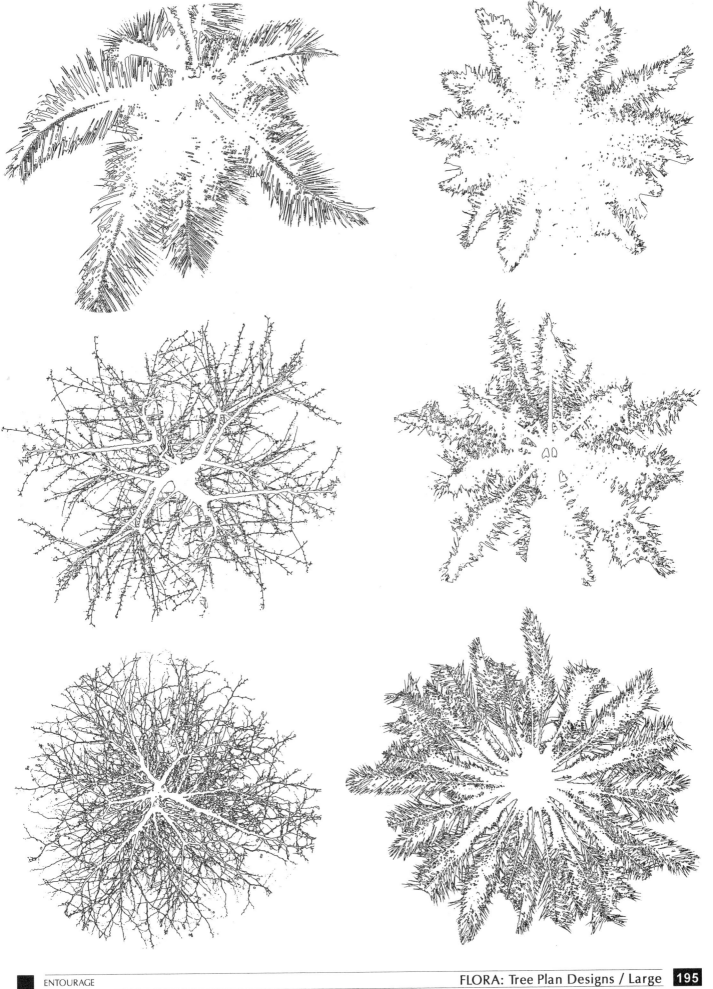

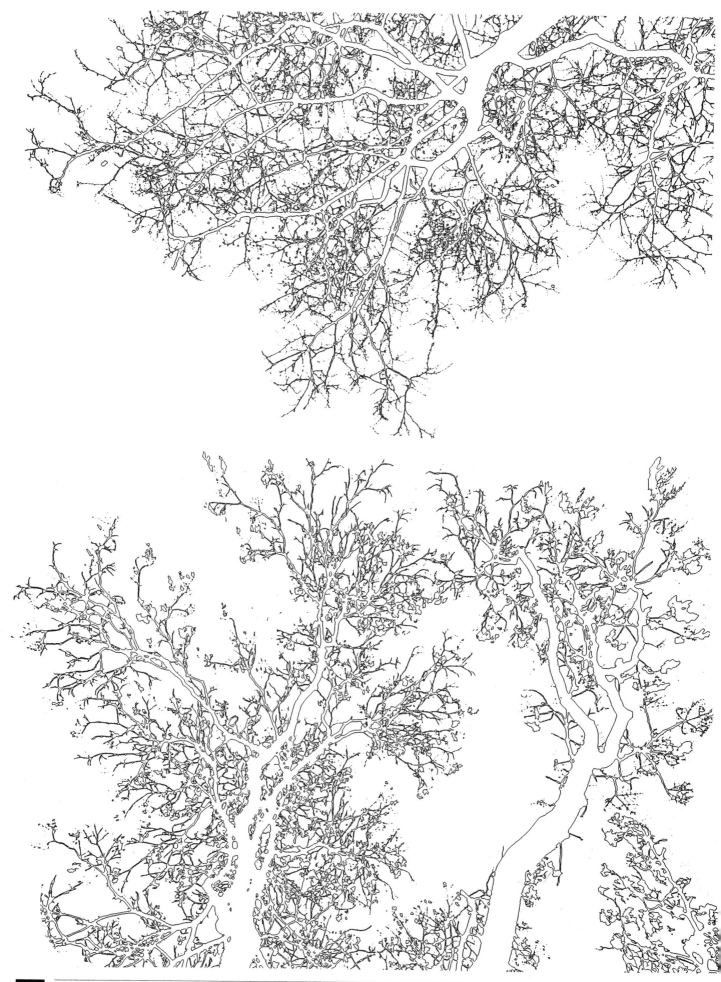

Deciduous trees are those that shed their leaves annually. One can see from the wide variety of leaf patterns and branch structures that there is an infinite number of ways to depict these trees. First, there is the structure of the tree as expressed in its trunk and branches. Then, there is the multitude of leaf patterns, and finally there is each individual person's own interpretation of all these elements. Drawing techniques vary from scribbles, abstract patterns, controlled textures, to drawing individual leaves among the trees in the foreground.

We see trees most often in profile, and they are easily photographed this way. Almost any hand-held camera can be used, and any ordinary outdoor film will be satisfactory. It is still a good Idea to use a high-speed film so you can use a fast shutter speed to stop any motion, such as wind, and get good depth of field to record the detail of the leaves.

The winter outline of a tree is useful for studying the structure, but lacks the scale of the foliage. These skeletal forms are used best in a drawing whenever it's important to keep the trees from obscuring detail on the structure; whenever a lighter treatment is desired; or when the scene depicted is in winter.

Sunny days are fine for illuminating the tree for pictures, but details may be obscured in the strong shadows. The most difficult aspect of photographing trees is to isolate the tree from its background of buildings, or worse, other trees. Try to isolate the tree against a contrasting bright or dark background. Spring and fall are the best times to photograph trees, as the structure of the trunk and limbs shows up more clearly.

Background trees and buildings are the most troublesome when trying to get a true photographic rendition of a tree specimen to use in a drawing.

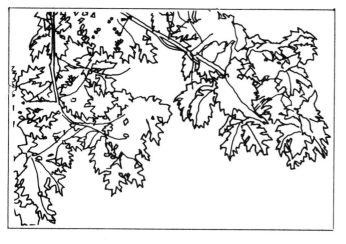
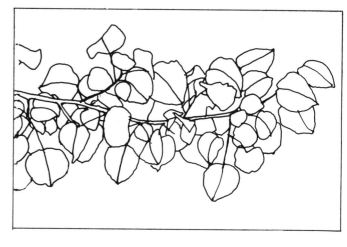
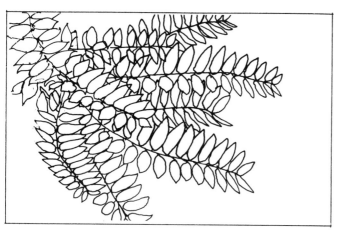
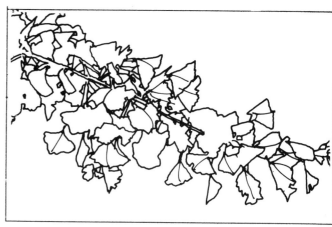
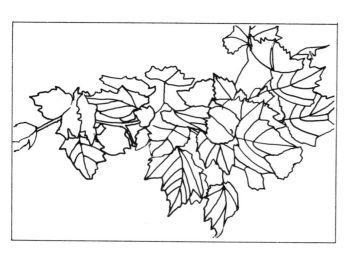
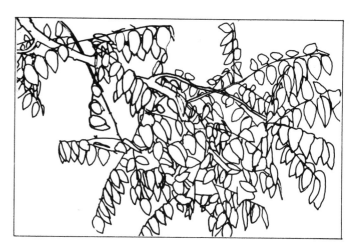
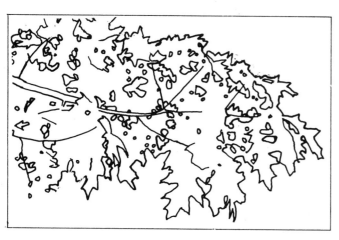
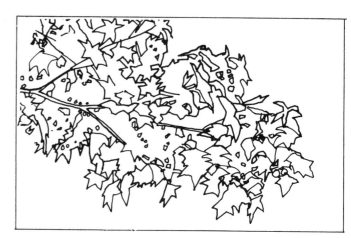

When you finally select a tree to use in a drawing you may want to sketch it in roughly on an overlay to make sure it will fit the scene. Then add the foliage that is the correct scale for the tree.

One way to make sure that you understand the structure of the leaf patterns is to take a few close-ups of the leaves and branches when initially photographing the tree. This will be very helpful later on, particularly if the tree is to be used in the foreground. Foreground tree and overhanging branches are one of the best techniques to establish depth and scale within a drawing. It is also a good device to frame the building.

■ There are two times a year when we
see trees as other than a large green mass
sitting on top of a trunk. That is in the spring
and fall, when there is a balance between
the leaves and the structure, and the effect
is much lighter in appearance. This is particularly useful when the trees are going to be
drawn in such a way that they cover parts of
the building. By using a lighter foliage, details
on the buildings will not be as obscured. It
also helps in relating the trees to the sky,
providing a lighter, brighter canopy rather
than a heavy dense one.

■ Trees seen in their winter outline are pure structure. They are skeletal in appearance, and often associated with the bleakness of the season. On the other hand, when shown in a drawing, they are the least obtrusive on the building, and allow it to be seen in more detail. Trees in winter outline are often used simply for their stark, simple appearance. At other times they are used to represent the winter season. It is important to make sure that all other elements, particularly the people, are dressed appropriately for the winter weather.

There are times when we want the fullness of the deciduous or palm tree without the heaviness usually associated with the mass of leaves. The use of the outline technique provides the answer. Any solid mass can be simplified into a single line representing the exterior surface, with the voids and branches outlined within. Simply reproduce any photograph of a tree as a line drawing rather than a screened photo. Photocopy it again using the "outline" function. The same can be done in a computer using an "autotrace" feature in a paint program.

■ Although this treatment may be used less frequently than others, it is a part of winter scenery and may be useful for special applications. There are several aspects of snow-covered conditions. One is where the tops of all the branches are coated with a thin layer of snow, while another has heavy snow piled on top of all the branches as a canopy. When used against a dark background, snow emphasizes the structure of the branches. When snow collects on lower shrubs, it is reminiscent of the flowering trees seen in the spring.

FLORA: Photographs / Snow-covered Trees

■ The evergreen tree is often associated with mountain locales, close to the timber-line. It is also found in smaller species, sprinkled among deciduous trees nearly everywhere. Since it never sheds its leaves, it is often used as an ornamental tree, and admired for its rustic beauty and color. We often associate evergreens with a conical-shaped profile, but they are far more varied in outline than the deciduous variety. The range in scale is extremely wide, and some of the oldest and tallest trees in existence are evergreens.

238 FLORA: Drawing by Robert McIlhargy (T)

■ Palm trees are very distinct in their appearance, and very difficult to depict accurately without the aid of reference material. The most common characteristic is the leafy branches radiating out from a central trunk high above the ground, and there are numerous variations within this mode. Some are slender, some are full; some are nearly symmetrical, while others appear haphazard. They typically are used to denote a tropical climate, but can be found elsewhere as isolated specimens. They are one of the most specialized tree shapes.

■ The use of plants in an interior drawing has a number of functions. It softens the edges of otherwise hard surfaces. It breaks down the scale of vast plain areas, and it relates to a human scale. Plants can be used in several areas of a drawing, depending on the function of the space. In the background they provide texture; in the foreground, depth and scale. Most renditions of plants have to be realistic in nature, particularly when shown in the foreground of a drawing. Reference sources should be used to accurately provide those details.

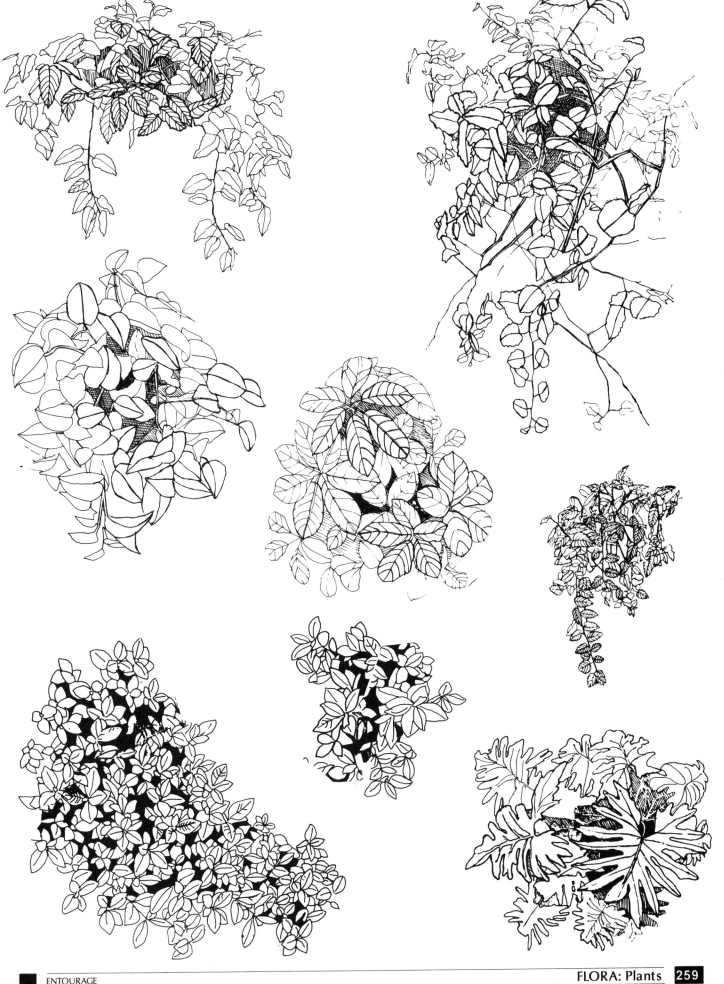

PART 4
■ Vehicles

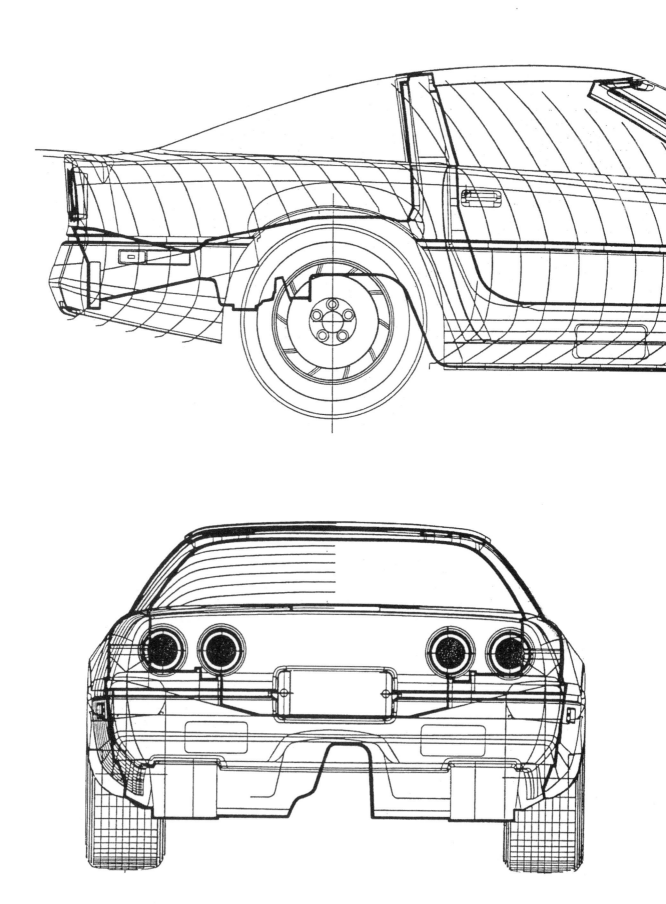

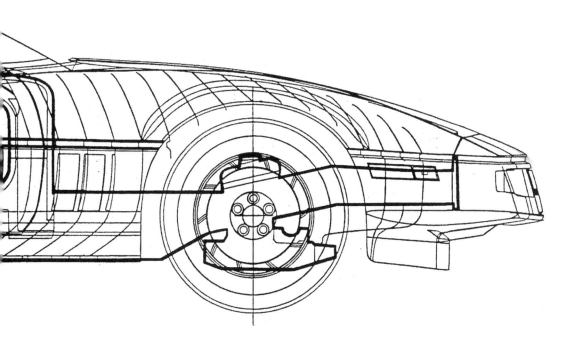

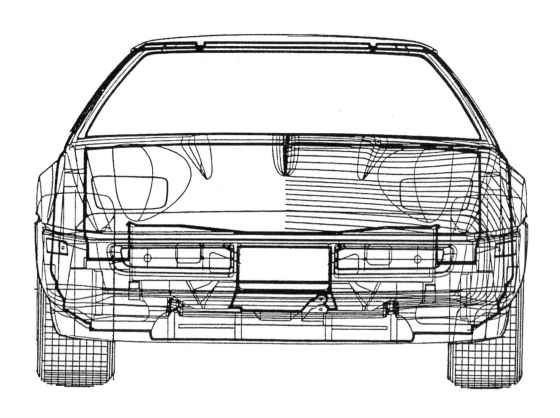

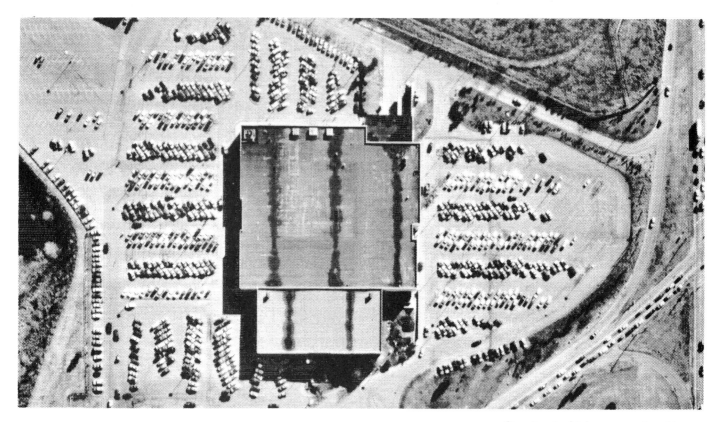

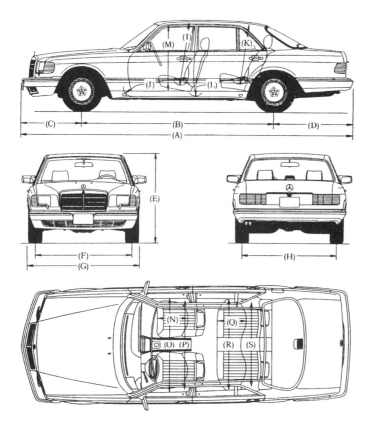

Our streets, highways, and parking lots are filled with vehicles of all descriptions. It is difficult to imagine any building that did not have some sort of vehicle nearby.

There are two aspects in which vehicles play a part in our drawings. The first and most common is the plan, side, front, and back view for two-dimensional representation. The second is the oblique angle used mainly for perspective views.

Most cars are similar in plan view with respect to the proportion of length to width, with minor dimensional variations depending on the make and model. Within this framework, however, they differ greatly in detail. Some cars change radically from year to year, some from decade to decade, and some have the same details as their predecessors. These are the classics.

Photographing cars is just as easy as photographing other elements, except of course for plan views. It is difficult to get directly above a car to get a true plan view. Usually, you will see more of one side than the other, but it will still give you a fairly accurate picture of the proportion and detailing of the car.

In recording elevational views, you need only be a distance of 20 to 30 feet away to get the proper viewpoint. A telephoto lens is the best way to avoid perspective foreshortening when photographing these views. Align yourself perpendicular to the surface of the vehicle to get the most accurate results, and keep the camera parallel to the plane of the vehicle.

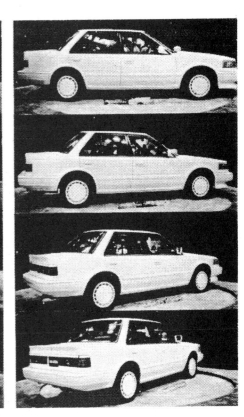

When photographing oblique views for perspective use, there is much more latitude. If you use either a normal or a telephoto lens, you will not get the distortion found with a wide angle lens, which allows you to get too close to the vehicle for the proper perspective.

Each year car manufacturers publish catalogs of their newest models, and these contain many photographs that are carefully staged to display the car's best design features. These are available at many showrooms, or at expositions held in major cities each year. Here, models are often exhibited on revolving platforms, where a series of views are available from a single vantage point. Many showroom vehicles are white, which photograph better than dark ones, and which show the finer details more clearly.

Another source, sometimes overlooked, is the scale model toy vehicle. The toy model is easier to photograph, particularly in plan view. If the model has sufficient detail, it would be difficult to tell whether the car was a real one photographed from 200 feet above the ground, or from 2 feet above the toy model.

■ A common element that is used on site plans, floor plans, and street elevations is the orthographic view of a vehicle. Plan views are shown in parking lots and garages, and it is very important that they be drawn to the correct scale. Most passenger vehicles of the same seating capacity are close to the same overall proportion, varying by only a few inches. However, there are larger variations between a compact car and a luxury sedan. Accurate reference material is plentiful on many models, and should be used when you depict vehicles in your drawings.

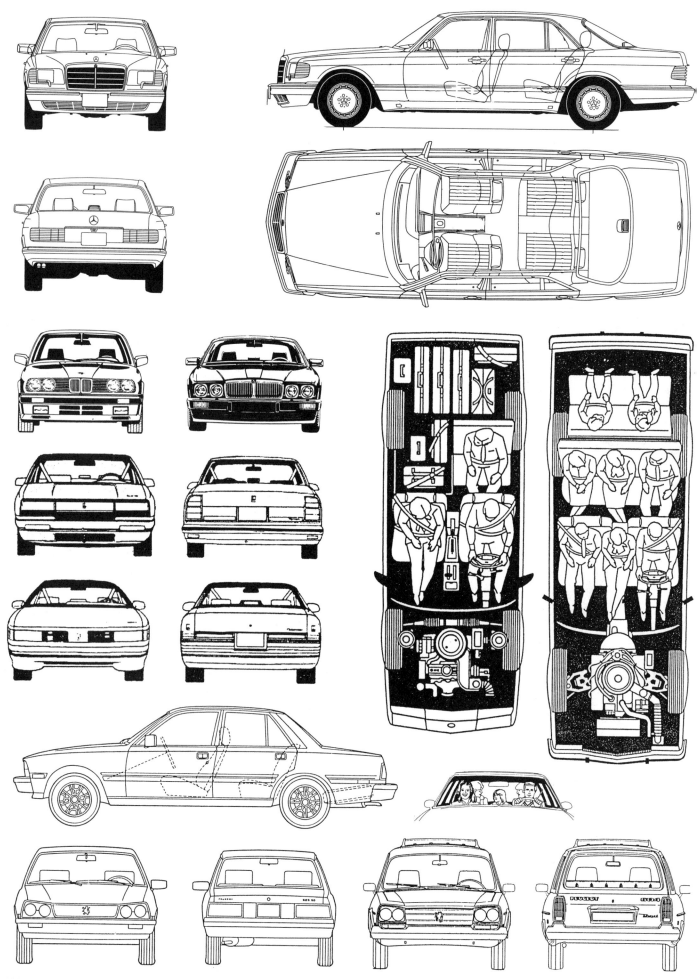

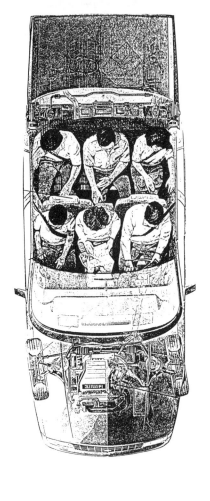

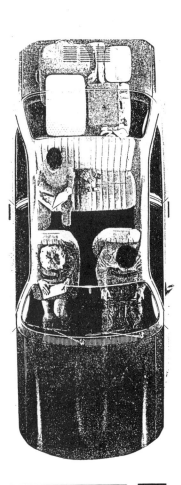

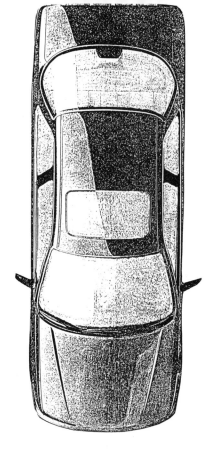

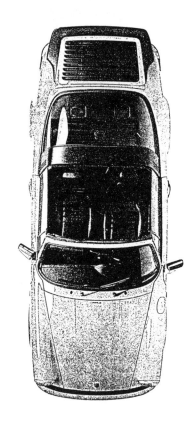

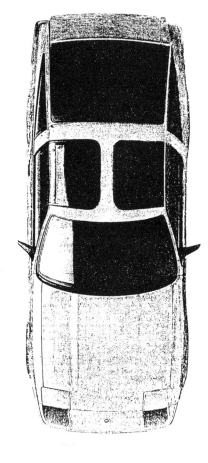

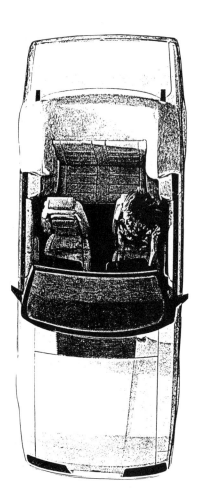

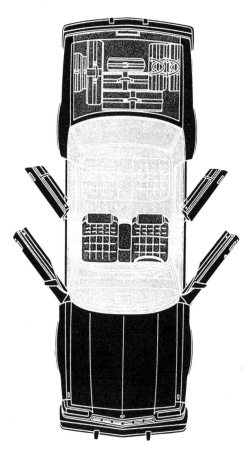

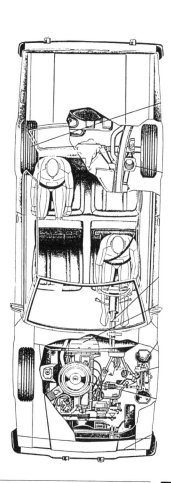

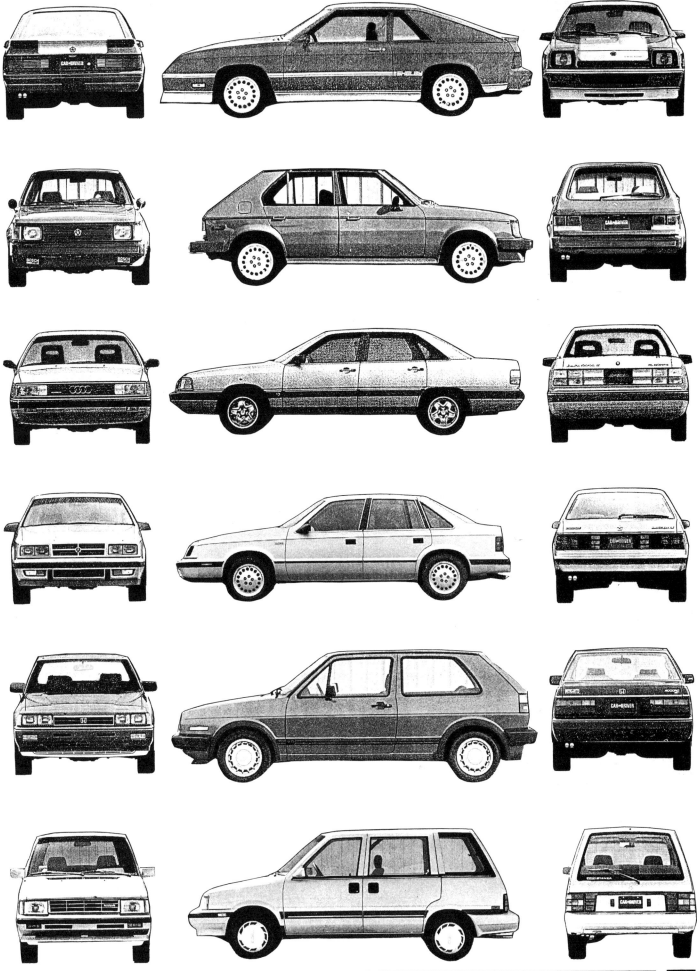

■ We see vehicles every day on streets, highways, and parking lots, and we have a keen sense of what they should look like when we see them in a drawing. Therefore, an improperly proportioned vehicle or one that is poorly drawn will be very noticeable in a drawing. Vehicles should have the proper scale and appropriate perspective angle to fit into the drawing. Vehicles that are placed in the foreground should have realist detail, so as not to be distracting. Those on the edge of the drawing should be headed into the drawing, not out of it.

1915 Buick

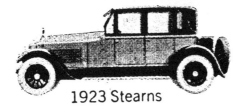
1923 Stearns

1931 Durant

1916 Oldsmobile

1924 Chandler

1932 Essex

1917 Oakland

1925 Locomobile

1933 Dodge

1918 Ford   Model "T"

1926 Kissel

1934 Chrysler

1919 Franklin

1927 Jordan

1935 Cadillac

1920 Chevrolet

1928 Ford Model "A"

1936 Terraplane

1921 Case

1929 Plymouth

1937 LaSalle

1922 Mercer

1930 Cord

1938 Ford

1939 Packard

1949 Ford

1957 Thunderbird

1940 Mercury

1950 Pontiac

1958 DeSoto

1941 Plymouth

1951 Nash Rambler

1959 Rambler

1942 Lincoln

1952 Plymouth

1960 Valiant

1943-44-45 Willys Jeep

1953 Mercury

1961 Willys

1946 DeSoto

1954 Chrysler

1962 Falcon

1947 Kaiser

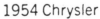

1955 Chevrolet

1963 Dodge

1948 Dodge

1956 Dodge

1964 Chevrolet

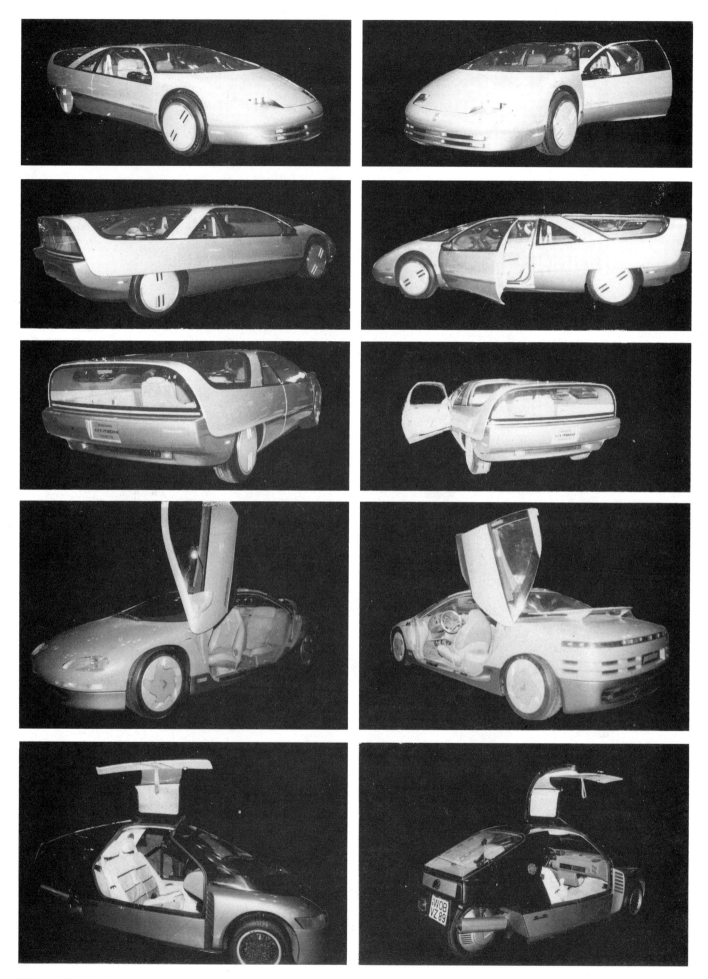

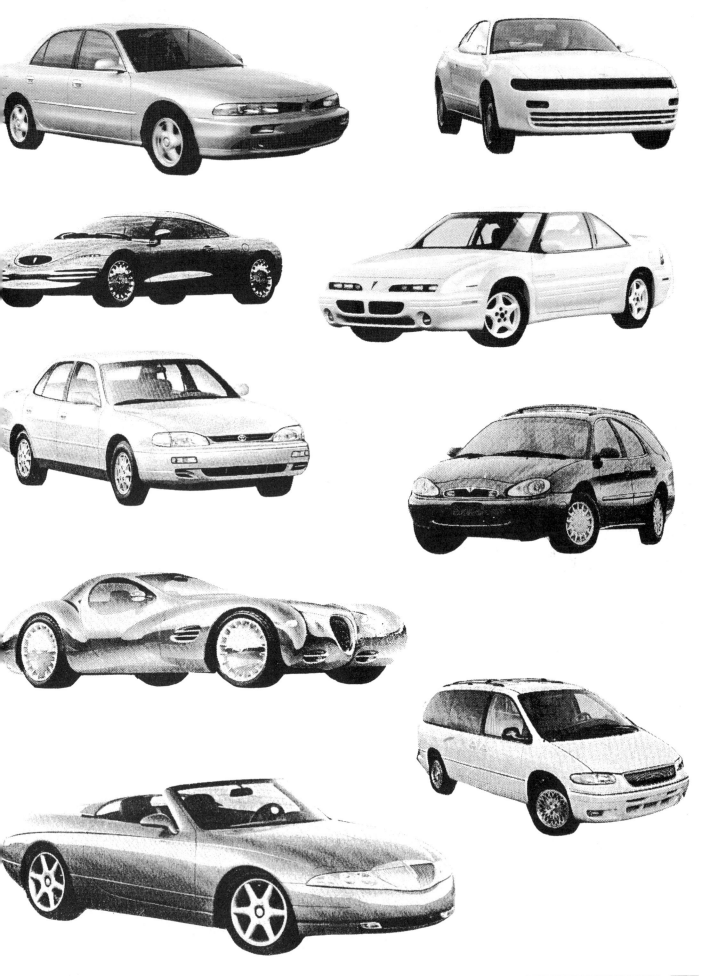

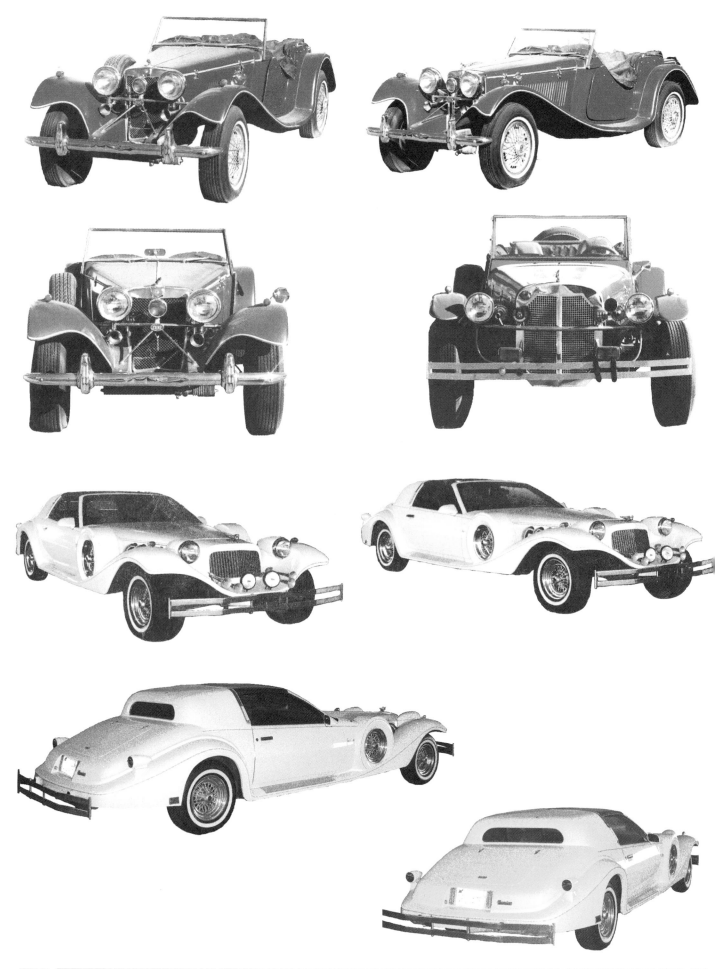

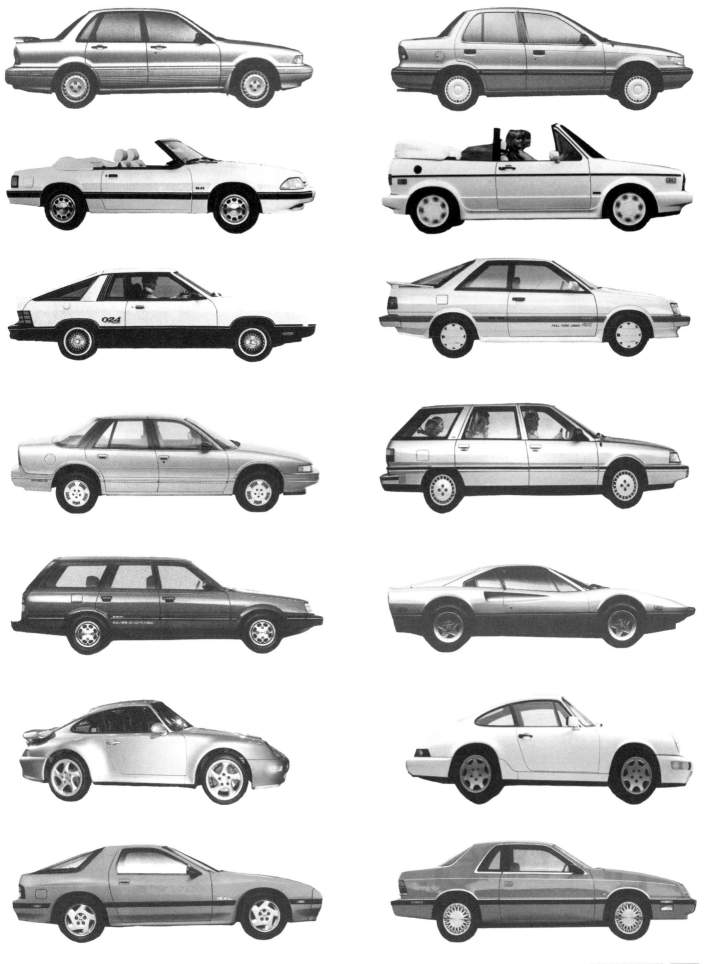

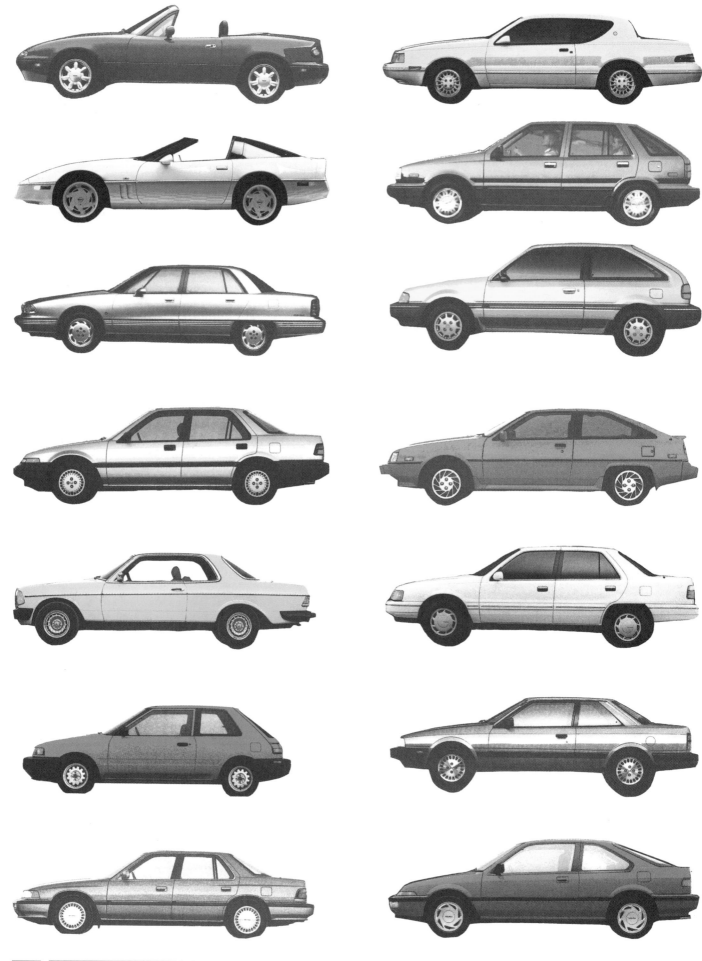

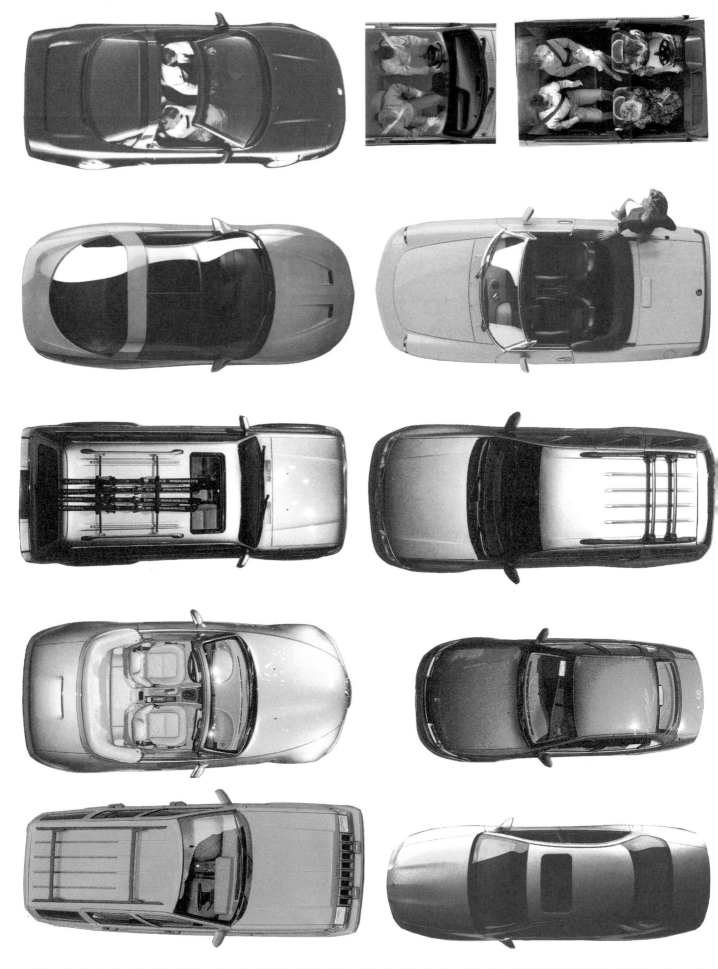

■ Marine activity is a specialty that can be found in every river and port city around the world. Since our heritage began with explorations by sea, these seaport areas were developed first. As expansion spread inland over the years, many of our water's edges were abandoned. However, there has been a resurgence of activity and renewal of all our natural resources, and waterfront projects are very popular and a source of renewed activity. Private residential developments have occurred also along waterways and in safe harbors.

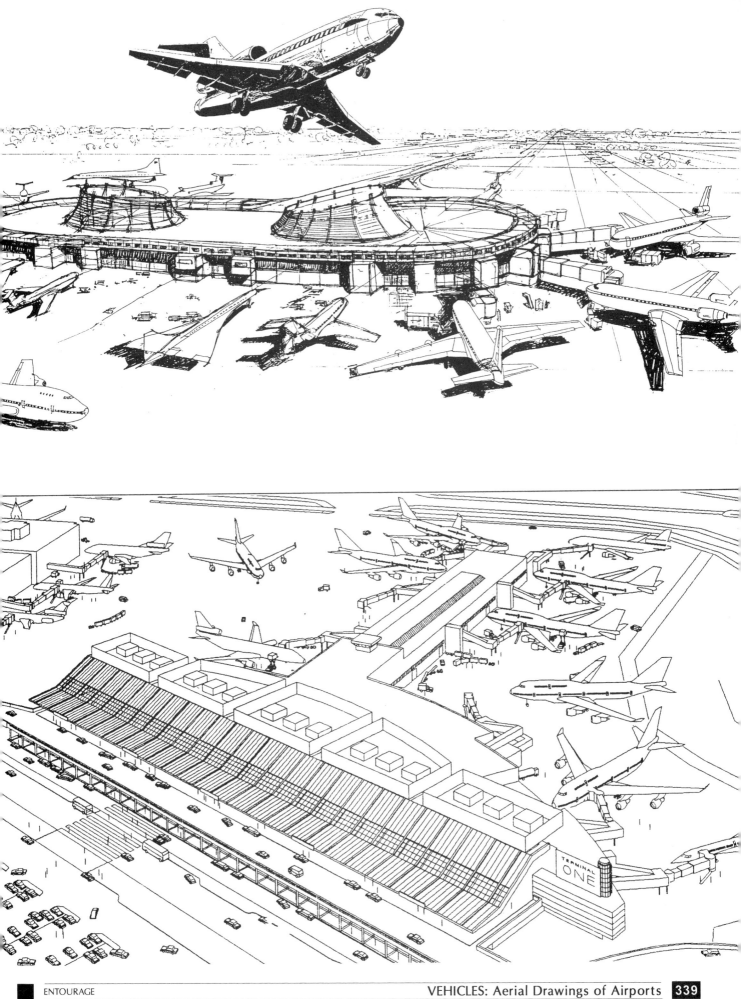

PART 5
■ Environment

■ Every project exists within a specific environment whether it's internal or external, and these environments are composed of a multitude of items both large and small. By selecting the proper elements of entourage, you can enhance the drawing, and create a lot more interest. These elements include objects and furniture, both interior and exterior, flags, fixtures, birds, airplanes, clouds, and all the incidentals that make up our world. These finishing touches are critical to the success of the drawing, and they also add interest f and scale.

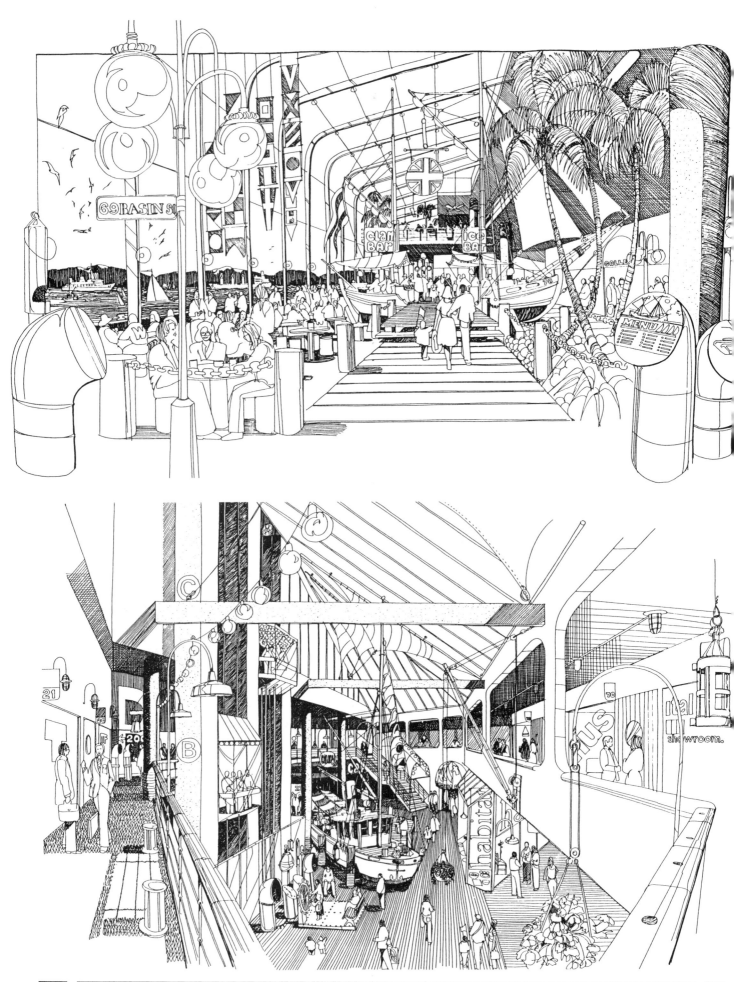

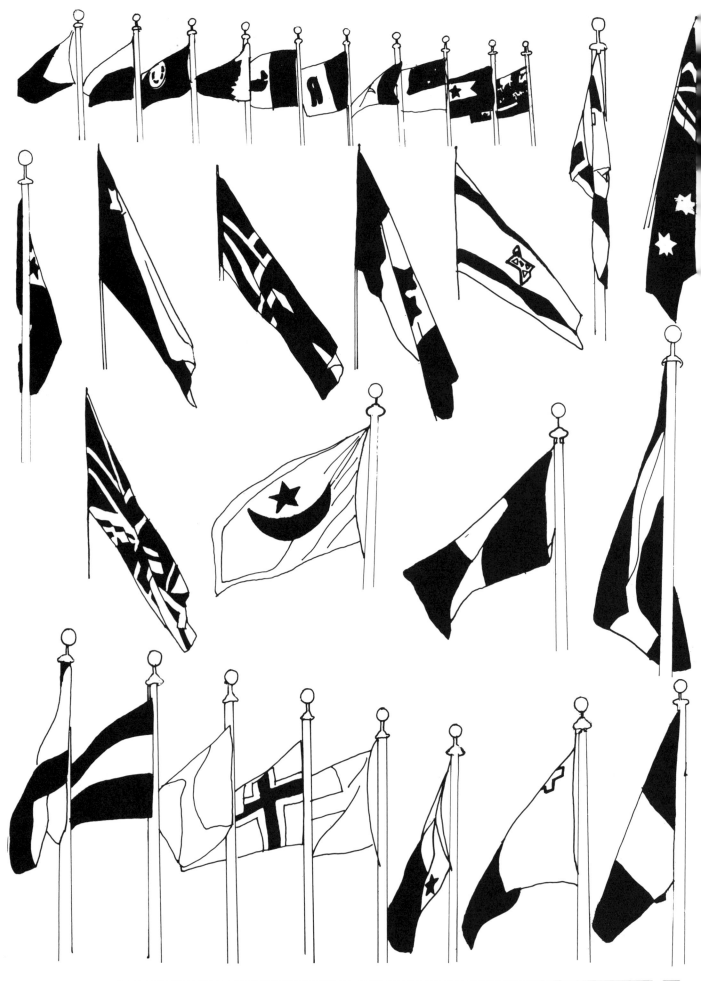

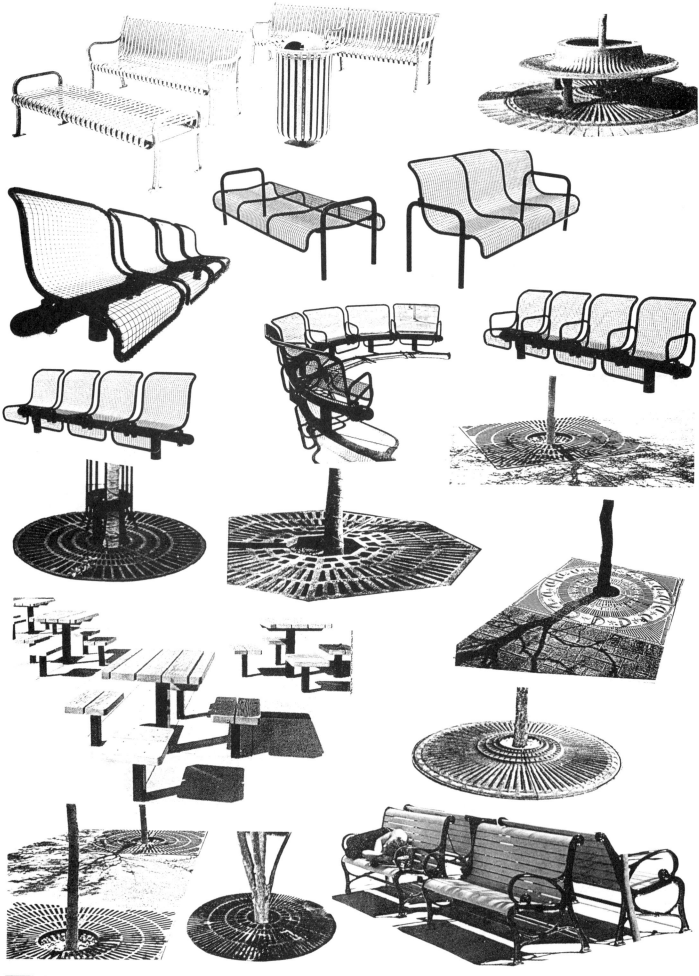

One of the most common and almost inescapable elements of entourage in an exterior drawing is the sky. The way it's treated in most cases will be a major consideration, although it may be quite different for every situation. Some drawings may not require much of a sky while in others it may be a vital element. Skies can enhance the building, or they can detract as well. Sky tones and textures can help balance a rendering by shifting the emphasis, or focusing the center of interest on certain parts of a building.

Our environment is composed of a multitude of items both natural and man-made. By studying and selecting the proper elements of the environment to complement the structure, you can enhance the drawing, and create a more interesting and believable rendition. These items include landscapes, interior objects, furniture, building materials, paving, flags, fixtures, clouds, and all the other natural elements that make up our world. These elements are essential to the success of the drawing, as they help to create a realistic appearance.

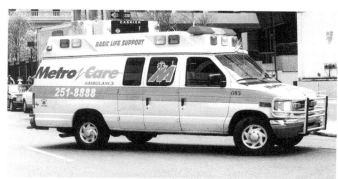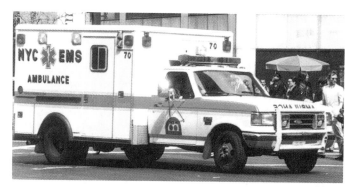